MW01010350

The Case For
Moral Clarity
Israel, Hamas and Gaza

Alan M. Dershowitz

CAMERA, the Committee for Accuracy in Middle East Reporting in America, is a national media-monitoring organization founded in 1982 that works to promote more accurate, balanced and complete coverage of Israel and the Middle East. Aware of the vital role of the mass media in shaping public perception and public policy, CAMERA seeks to educate both journalists and news consumers about the complex issues related to achievement of peace in the Middle East. CAMERA is a non-profit, tax-exempt organization under section 501(c)(3) of the United States Internal Revenue Code.

Published by
The Committee for Accuracy in Middle East Reporting in America
CAMERA
P.O. Box 35040
Boston, MA 02135

Book design: Susan Rubin

Cover illustration: The computer-generated cartoon on the cover has been widely circulated on the internet. It displays no copyright and is anonymous. We have made considerable efforts to try to discover its source so that we can give him or her appropriate credit. If the person responsible for creating it comes forward, we would like to give him the appropriate credit in any further editions of the book. In the meantime we express our great appreciation to him or her for creating a newsworthy and important contribution to the marketplace of ideas.

Photos: P. 3 MEMRI screen capture, P. 6 "The Case for Israel" screen capture, P. 8 © Reuters Photographer/Reuters, P. 9 AFP PHOTO/Mahmud HAMS, P. 11 Jack Guez/AFP/Getty Images, P. 15 CNN screen capture, P. 18 missile launcher http://www.ruleta.nazory.cz/gaza_strip_11.php, P. 22 Muqawamah website 2.27.08, P. 28 PoliticalCartoons.com, P. 34 Professor Iain Scobbie BBC video screen capture, P. 41 BBC news 1.9.09 screen capture , P. 42 Daylife.com

This book is warmly dedicated to the brave residents of Sderot who have endured rocket attacks without losing their will to live or desire for peace. It is also dedicated, with sadness, to innocent Palestinian victims of the Hamas tactic of using civilians as human shields.

My appreciation goes to Susan Rubin, who has brilliantly designed and coordinated this book in a very short amount of time, and to Joel Pollak, who has helped me with the research.

CONTENTS

Introduction

Hamas's tactic of playing Russian roulette with the lives of Israeli children by firing thousands of rockets at a million Israelis, while employing human shields in order to maximize Palestinian civilian casualties, is pure evil. The Israeli decision to respond to this unlawful and immoral provocation by targeting the terrorists and their rockets is pure self-defense, authorized by international law, the United Nations Charter and universally accepted moral principles. Yet most of the world remained silent about, and many even supported, the Hamas evil tactic, while most of the world condemned Israel's entirely reasonable response.

When the media began to cover this latest war started by Hamas, and Israel's response to it, I noticed a strong media bias against Israel. Sometimes it was quite deliberate, but sometimes it was simply the result of the media's understandable focus on showing dead and injured victims, particularly children. I decided that it was important to present a fuller perspective in the court of public opinion. Accordingly I set out to write a series of Op-Eds, defending Israel's right to protect its citizens by proportional military action. Over the course of the war I published my writings in the *Wall Street Journal, The Christian Science Monitor, the Los Angeles Times, the Miami Herald, The New York Times,* the *Washington Times, The Canada Post,* the *Huffington Post,* the *Jerusalem Post,* Frontpagemag and other print and online media. I also participated in interviews and debates on CNN and BBC. The response was overwhelming. I received numerous emails and letters imploring me to circulate my views more widely, since the perspective I presented in my writings and appearances was very much a minority view in the media. When cease fires were finally declared, I decided to publish revised and updated versions of these essays and several new ones written especially for this volume in a short book, in order to make them more widely available in an easily accessible format, and to respond to the often erroneous and biased misinformation that passes for objective description.

This short book asks why so much of the world has been so morally bankrupt—so "eyeless in Gaza" when it comes to the conflict between Hamas and Israel. Why has there been so little moral clarity over this conflict between good and evil? Why does the media not do a better job of explaining that the dead Palestinian children it shows the world were killed because they were deliberately placed in harm's way by Hamas precisely in order to create these horrible images? Why is a double standard applied to Israeli self-defense actions? Why are the usual standards of criticism not applied to Hamas's double war crimes? Why are there so many more protests and so much more rage when the Israeli Army accidentally kills human shields in defense of its own children than when Muslims murder Muslims in cold blood and in much larger numbers throughout the world? Why is terrorism justified by so many only when it is directed at Israeli civilians? Why is so much of the world so wrong when it comes to Israel?

Let me begin with a brief chronology that places the Gaza conflict in context.

On October 2, 2001, President George W. Bush announced that the United States supported the creation of a Palestinian state. It was a major milestone for the Palestinian cause, since no previous American administration had officially acknowledged a Palestinian state as an explicit goal of U.S. foreign policy. The announcement was all the more remarkable, given that the U.S. was still reeling in the wake of 9/11, and that Palestinian extremists were still using terror against Israelis to achieve their goals. Bush's announcement offered a unique opportunity to Palestinians to end the violence and begin building a new future. Hamas's response came a few weeks later, when it fired the first Qassam rocket at the Israeli town of Sderot. The Hamas website proudly proclaimed: "The Zionist army is afraid that the Palestinians will increase the range of the new rockets, placing the towns and villages in the [Zionist] entity in danger."[1]

It was only the first of thousands of rockets that Hamas and other Palestinian terror organizations would fire in their relentless effort to kill Jews and destroy the peace process.

Rocket and mortar fire from the Gaza Strip peaked in late 2004 and early 2005. There was a brief halt in March 2005, in the aftermath of Mahmoud Abbas's victory in the Palestinian presidential elections, and an agreement signed by the various Palestinian factions in Cairo to halt violence. Hamas and other organizations merely used the lull to re-arm, however. In August of that year, Israel carried out its "disengagement" from Gaza, voluntarily withdrawing thousands of settlers and soldiers, leaving twenty-one communities behind and completely ending the Israeli presence there. The hope was that Palestinians would use the end of Israeli occupation to build Gaza's economy and prepare it for political independence, along with the West Bank, as part of a Palestinian state. Private donors stepped in to buy the Israeli greenhouses that had been left behind, and hand them over to the Palestinian Authority. James Wolfenson, the former head of the World Bank, contributed $500,000 of his own money to the purchase.[2]

But almost immediately after the disengagement, Hamas and other terror organizations renewed their rocket fire, launching a barrage of rockets at the Israeli towns of Sderot and Ashqelon. The immediate trigger was an accident during a Hamas "victory rally," in which a truck filled with weapons exploded in a Gaza refugee camp, killing 19 Palestinians.[3] There was little media focus on, and no demonstrations against, these largely civilian deaths.

Rocket fire continued throughout the months that followed, though Israel was no longer occupying Gaza at all. In November 2005, Israel signed an agreement with the Palestinian Authority to open the Rafah Crossing on the Egypt-Gaza border. The agreement was part of an effort to encourage trade and economic development in Gaza, and to increase the responsibilities of the Palestinian government for the welfare of the Palestinian people. And, indeed, the Rafah Crossing remained open throughout the first half of 2006.[4] The border remained open despite Hamas's victory in the Palestinian legislative elections in January 2006, which caused deep worry in Israel and throughout the international community. The Middle East Quartet—comprised of the European Union, United Nations, United States and Russia—warned the new Palestinian government that further aid would be conditional on its "commitment to the principles of non-violence, recognition of Israel, and acceptance of previous agreements and obligations."[5] With several weeks to go before the new Palestinian government would be sworn in, Hamas had time to consider those reasonable conditions. And it rejected every one of them. That decision, in turn, prompted the Quartet, and Israel, to cut off financial assistance to the Palestinian Authority, though Israel continued to supply electricity and water to Gaza.

Hamas had a chance to reconsider. Instead, it resumed its attacks. Only one rocket was launched against Israel in January 2006, while Palestinian elections were under way. But in February alone, 47 rockets were fired. By June, Hamas and other groups had launched hundreds of Qassams, as well as an Iranian-made Grad rocket. On June 25, Hamas launched an attack inside Israel, having tunneled under the border near the Kerem Shalom ("Vineyard of Peace") border crossing. In the ensuing battle, Hamas kidnapped an Israeli soldier named Gilad Shalit, whom it continues to hold incomunicado today in violation of the principles of the Third Geneva Convention. Following the attack, Israel attacked terrorist targets in Gaza and closed the Rafah Crossing. The closure was not an attempt to punish Palestinians for the election result five months before, but was the direct

According to a translation by MEMRI, the Middle East Media Research Institute, on February 29, 2008, Fathi Hammad, a Hamas Member of the Palestinian Legislative Council, stated:

"For the Palestinian people, death has become an industry, at which women excel, and so do all the people living on this land. The elderly excel at this, and so do the mujahideen and the children. This is why they have formed human shields of the women, the children, the elderly, and the mujahideen, in order to challenge the Zionist bombing machine. It is as if they were saying to the Zionist enemy: 'We desire death like you desire life.'"

consequence of Hamas's attack on Israel, and was deemed necessary to protect Israel's security.

Even after Hamas abducted Shalit, the Gaza borders were not completely closed. The Rafah Crossing was open for 83 days over the next year, and some movement of people and goods—albeit restricted—was allowed. Throughout this time, rocket fire from the Gaza Strip continued to terrorize Israeli civilians. Still, the international community gave the Palestinian leaders another chance to meet the basic demands it had issued in January 2006. But the two main Palestinian factions—Fatah, which controlled the executive, and Hamas, which controlled the legislature—began fighting openly with each other.

After extensive negotiations, the two parties agreed to form a unity government, which took place in March 2007. But the rockets continued to rain down—reaching a record high of 257 in May 2007—and in June 2007, Hamas launched a military coup against the Fatah executive, driving its leaders out of Gaza and killing over 100 of their fellow Palestinians, including many civilians. Again, there was little media focus and no protest marches. With the entire territory under its iron-fisted control, Hamas increased rocket attacks against Israel, with other Palestinian terror organizations joining in. These attacks accelerated dramatically after Israel and the exiled Palestinian Authority leaders—still legally governed by Fatah, in the eyes of the international community—signed an agreement in Annapolis, Maryland, in November 2007, pledging to work towards a two-state solution.

It was only after Hamas's illegal and illegitimate coup, and the heavy rocket attacks that followed, that Israel imposed more extensive sanctions on Gaza. In January 2008—two years after Hamas took power, and after thousands of rockets and mortars had fallen on Israel's southern towns—Israel began restricting fuel and electricity to Gaza, in accordance with a nuanced ruling by Israel's High Court of Justice. Still, it continued to allow fuel and humanitarian aid to enter, and allowed Palestinians to enter Israel to receive medical treatment in Israeli hospitals. Israel did not want ordinary Palestinians to suffer, and did all that it could to alleviate their living conditions while reducing Hamas's ability to function as a terrorist regime.

And yet Hamas continued to smuggle weapons into Gaza via underground tunnels

Hamas legislator Fathi Hammad on Al-Aqsa TV lauds Palestinian use of "human shields."

3

on the Egyptian border. More than 2,000 rockets and mortars were launched from Gaza into Israel in the first six months of 2008. Finally, in June, Israel and Hamas began an Egyptian-brokered "period of calm," during which rocket fire, though greatly reduced, continued to strike Israeli towns. In December 2008, Hamas unilaterally declared that it would resume its attacks with full force—and it promptly did so when the period of calm expired, forcing Israel to respond with Operation Cast Lead.

When these facts are examined, it is clear that Palestinian rocket attacks against Israeli civilians were not a response to Gaza's increasing isolation, but the cause thereof. The first rocket attacks began in October 2001, precisely when the world was most eager to create a viable Palestinian state. They continued even after Israel pulled its army and its settlements out of Gaza in 2005. They accelerated after Hamas took power in 2006, increasing dramatically in 2007 when Israel and the Palestinian Authority resolved to renew negotiations towards a two-state solution. And the attacks were renewed in December 2008 when Hamas unilaterally declared that it would refuse to extend a period of calm that had been accepted by both sides.

The sanctions that were imposed on Gaza—not only by Israel, but the world—were the direct result of Hamas's refusal to meet the international community's basic, reasonable demands: stop terror, recognize Israel, and respect previous agreements. Even after Hamas took power in the 2006 elections, the Gaza borders remained relatively open, until Hamas escalated the conflict by abducting Gilad Shalit in June 2006, overthrowing the legitimate Palestinian executive in a violent coup in June 2007, and launching more and more rockets and mortars at Israeli civilians. Hamas brought about the isolation of Gaza because it is neither interested in peace nor in the welfare of the Palestinian people. Instead, it is fanatically committed to the destruction of Israel itself, a goal it pursues using weapons and funding it receives from the Islamic Republic of Iran, for which Hamas acts as a proxy and whose ambitions of regional domination it serves.

Israelis and Palestinians have the same right to live in peace. Hamas and its fellow terror organizations deny that right, and disrupt every attempt to move the peace process forward. That is why the Gaza War was a tragic necessity. That is why the conflict continues. Only when the leaders—all of the leaders—of the Palestinian people are prepared to meet the world's basic demands will peace become a real possibility.

Only when the Palestinian people and their elected leaders want to establish their own state more than they want to destroy the Jewish state, will the two-state solution become a reality.

It is against this backdrop that I began to write my series of Op-Eds in December of 2008, January of 2009, to the present.

---

[1] Hamas website, quoted in "Rocket threat from the Gaza Strip, 2000-2007," Intelligence and Terrorism Information Center at the Israel Intelligence Heritage and Commemoration Center (IICC), Dec. 2007, 33-34.

[2] CNN.com, "Gaza settlers' greenhouses to be handed to Palestinians," Aug. 12, 2005, <http://www.cnn.com/2005/WORLD/meast/08/12/gaza/index.html>.

[3] IICC, ibid., 40.

[4] B'Tselem, "The Gaza Strip after disengagement," accessed Feb. 15, 2009, <http://btselem.org/English/Gaza_Strip/>.

[5] Statement by Middle East Quartet, Jan. 30, 2006, <http://www.un.org/News/Press/docs/2006/sg2104.doc.htm>.

Chapter One
Israel, Hamas and Moral Idiocy

When Israel first responded to Hamas's decision to end the cease fire and send a barrage of rockets into southern Israel, the Christian Science Monitor *asked for my assessment of the situation. This is what I wrote. It was published on December 31, 2008.*

Israel's decision to take military action against Hamas rocket attacks targeting its civilian population has been long in coming. I vividly recall a visit my wife and I took to the Israeli city of Sderot on March 20 of 2008. Over the past four years, Palestinian terrorists—in particular, Hamas and Islamic Jihad—have fired more than 2,000 rockets at this civilian area, which is home to mostly poor and working-class people.

The rockets are designed exclusively to maximize civilian deaths, and some have barely missed school yards, kindergartens, hospitals, and school buses. But others hit their targets, killing more than a dozen civilians since 2001, including in February 2008 a father of four who had been studying at the local university. These anti-civilian rockets have also injured and traumatized countless children.[6] They are fired primarily on school days at a time of day when the schoolchildren are arriving at their classes.

In most parts of the world, the first words learned by toddlers are "mommy" and "daddy." In Sderot, they are "red alert." The police chief of Sderot showed me hundreds of rocket fragments that had been recovered. Many bore the name of the terrorist group that had fired the deadly missiles. Although firing deliberately to kill civilians is a war crime, the terrorists who fired at the civilians of Sderot were proud enough of their crimes to "sign" their murderous weapons. They know that in the real world in which we live, they will never be prosecuted for their murders and attempted murders.

I spoke in front of these rockets [excerpts of my talk appear on page 6]. I also conversed with many long-suffering residents who were demanding that their nation take action to protect them. But Israel's postoccupation military options were limited, since Hamas deliberately fires its deadly rockets from densely populated urban areas, and the Israeli army has a strict policy of trying to avoid civilian casualties. This, in a nutshell, is the dilemma faced by democracies with a high level of morality.

The firing of rockets at civilians from densely populated civilian areas is the newest tactic in the war between terrorists who love death and democracies that love life. The terrorists have learned how to exploit the morality of democracies against those who do not want to kill civilians, even enemy civilians.

The attacks on Israeli citizens have little to do with what Israel does or does not do. They have everything to do with an ideology that despises—and openly seeks to destroy—the Jewish state. Consider that rocket attacks increased substantially after Israel disengaged from Gaza in 2005, and they accelerated further after Hamas seized control last year.

In the past months, a shaky cease-fire, organized by Egypt, was in effect. Hamas agreed to stop the rockets and Israel agreed to stop taking military action against Hamas terrorists in the Gaza

continued on page 8

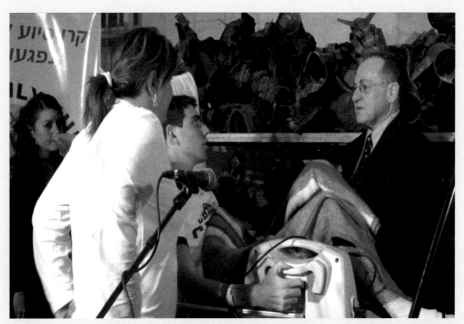

Alan Dershowitz in front of Hamas rocket shells with young man injured by Hamas rockets in Sderot.

I arrived in Sderot on the Jewish holiday of Purim, which commemorates the Jewish victory over the evil Persian, Hamen, who had plotted to kill all the Jews of Persia. Despite the threat of rocket attacks, the Purim festivities were in full swing at the Yeshiva, headed by my cousin Dov Fendel. The students were dancing and singing so loud that the person in charge of security was worried they would not hear the "red alert" siren that signaled an incoming Kassam rocket. The residents of Sderot have 15 seconds from the launch of the rocket to run into a shelter. The rule is that everyone must always be within 15 seconds of a shelter, regardless of what they are doing. Shelters are everywhere, but the aged and the physically challenged often have difficulty making it to safety. On the night I was in Sderot, a rocket landed nearby, but there had been no "red alert." The warning system is far from foolproof.

I was in Sderot to show solidarity with its residents, who are on the front line in the war against terrorism. I made a speech to the residents (and others who watched by videoconference) from the police station, standing in front of hundreds of rocket fragments that had been recovered.

As I spoke, I stood beside a teenage boy who had been seriously injured by a rocket that blew off his younger brother's leg. I also stood near a grieving mother whose 4 year old daughter had been killed by a rocket and a man whose wife and two children had been murdered by terrorists. The tension was palpable, as car alarms sounded, frightening only those of us who could not distinguish it from a red alert.

This is what I said to the victims of terrorism:

I am here tonight to stand in solidarity with you against those who are trying to kill your children—and against those whose silence in the face of these war crimes serves to encourage terrorists to persist in their murderous means.

Hamas is playing one of the most despicably immoral and dangerous games of Russian roulette with the lives of Jewish children. 8000 rockets aimed at civilians... not a single one of them has a legitimate military purpose. Every one of them is an unlawful, anti-personnel, terrorist bomb. Where is the United Nations? Where are the human rights organizations? Where are those that claim to speak out on behalf of human rights and against international war crimes? These are war crimes against Jewish people, against the people of Israel, against children, against women…[W]e hear [that]… only 9 people have died, as if 9 people dying is not enough. Every single person who dies is a generation missing. Children and grandchildren and great grandchildren. And what about the people so traumatized and so injured and so wounded…. The world is waiting for one of those rockets to hit a school bus, … an ambulance … a hospital. Then the world will say it's ok for Israel to respond.

… What other democracy in the world would wait … wait until that horrible disaster occurs. It's inevitable. It's the law of averages. It is absolutely amazing that greater catastrophes have not befallen this city. This brave city. This embattled city.

I'm not here to suggest what Israel ought to do. Those are tactical decisions but as a human rights lawyer I can tell you this.

Israel has every right … legally and morally to do whatever it takes to prevent another rocket from landing on Sderot … Israel holds itself to a higher moral standard. Israel does not set out to kill civilians.

No country in the world fighting a comparable battle against terrorism, rockets, the threat of nuclear weapons from Iran … has ever complied with a higher standard of the rule of law, a higher standard of human rights and has had a better ratio of combatants to civilians killed. Most recently when Israel has used targeted killings against terrorists, it's ratio has been incredible. One civilian for every 30 combatants killed. And yet the world continues to complain … All we hear from the United Nations commissions on human rights and the General Assembly … all we hear is criticism of Israel. All we hear from the International Court is why did you have to build the security barrier? Why didn't you just let terrorists come and kill you? Israel must move more quickly to reinforce the homes, it must move more quickly to take whatever technological steps, no matter how expensive, to give more advance notice to protect its citizens because they are our heroes. They are the people that are on the forefront of Israel's survival.

You cannot fight a war against terrorists who hide behind civilians and use civilians as human shields without occasionally killing a civilian. And when Israel accidentally kills a civilian it goes into a collective state of sitting shiva. It regrets it. It bemoans it. It hates the idea that it has to kill a civilian. Golda Meir put it so well 30 years ago when she said to Palestinian terrorists "we can perhaps forgive you for killing our children, but we can never forgive you for making us kill your children." And remember that's Hamas's goal. Hamas has two goals. It wants to kill as many Israeli children and civilians as it can, and it wants Israel to kill as many Palestinian civilians and children as is possible, because it regards these children, these Palestinian children, as Martyrs.
…

Terrorism has been rewarded by the United Nations. Terrorism has been rewarded by Amnesty International. Terrorism has been rewarded by Human Rights Watch—all of which condemn the victims and support the terrorists. They are winning and that is why Sderot is such an important symbol, not only for Israel, but for the world. It is the symbol for resisting terrorism around the world. If Sderot is allowed to be victimized today, it will be Tel Aviv tomorrow. It will be Haifa the day after tomorrow. And it will be Toronto next year. Because terrorism doesn't stop at national borders. It is not directed only against Israel. It is directed against the civilized Western world.
…

We are you. And you are us. We will never, ever abandon you.

continued from page 5

Strip. The cease-fire itself was morally dubious and legally asymmetrical.

Israel, in effect, was saying to Hamas: If you stop engaging in the war crime of targeting our innocent civilians, we will stop engaging in the entirely lawful military acts of targeting your terrorists. Under the cease-fire, Israel reserved the right to engage in self-defense actions such as attacking terrorists who were in the process of firing rockets at its civilians.

Just before the hostilities began, Israel offered a carrot and a stick: it reopened a checkpoint to allow humanitarian aid to enter Gaza. It had closed the point of entry after the checkpoint had been targeted by Gazan rockets. (On several prior occasions, Hamas rockets had targeted Israel points of entry through which aid had been provided. It was as if Hamas was deliberately trying to manufacture a humanitarian crisis.) Israel's prime minister, Ehud Olmert, also issued a stern, final warning to Hamas that unless it stopped the rockets, there would be a full-scale military response.

This is the way Reuters reported it:

> "Israel reopened border crossings with the Gaza Strip on Friday, a day after Prime Minister warned militants there to stop firing rockets or they would pay a heavy price. Despite the movement of relief supplies, militants fired about a dozen rockets and mortar shafts from Gaza at Israel on Friday. One accidentally struck a house in Gaza, killing two Palestinian sisters, ages 5 and 13. [T]he deliveries could ease the tensions that might have led to a military action to end the rocket attacks. Palestinian workers at the crossings said fuel had arrived for Gaza's main power plant and about a hundred trucks loaded with grain, humanitarian aid and other goods were expected during the day."

Despite the opening of the crossings, the Hamas rockets continued, and Israel kept its word, implementing a carefully prepared targeted air attack against Hamas targets.

Hamas combatants firing from area with children all around.

On Sunday, I spoke to the air force general, now retired, who worked on the planning of the attack. He told me of the intelligence and planning that had gone into preparing for the contingency that the military option might become necessary. The Israeli air force had pinpointed with precision the exact locations of Hamas structures in an effort to minimize civilian casualties.

Even Hamas sources have acknowledged that the vast majority of those killed [in the initial air attack] have been Hamas terrorists, though some civilian casualties are inevitable when, as BBC's Rushdi Abou Alouf—who is certainly not pro-Israel—reported, "The Hamas security compounds are in the middle of the city." Indeed, his home balcony was just 20 meters away from a compound he saw bombed.

There have been three types of international response to the Israeli military actions against the Hamas rockets. Not surprisingly, Iran, Hamas, and other knee-jerk Israel-bashers have argued that the Hamas rocket attacks against Israeli civilians are entirely legitimate and that the Israeli counterattacks are war crimes.

Palestinian human shields gather around and on top of a house in the northern Gaza Strip town of Jabalya late 18 November 2006 after Israeli troops ordered the house's occupants to leave before an airstrike.

Equally unsurprising is the response of the United Nations, the European Union, Russia, and others who, at least when it comes to Israel, see a moral and legal equivalence between terrorists who target civilians and a democracy that responds by targeting the terrorists.

And finally, there is the United States and a few other nations that place the blame squarely on Hamas for its unlawful and immoral policy of using its own civilians as human shields, behind whom they fire rockets at Israeli civilians.

The most dangerous of the three responses is not the Iranian-Hamas absurdity, which is largely ignored by thinking and moral people, but the United Nations and European Union response, which equates the willful murder of civilians with legitimate self-defense pursuant to Article 51 of the United Nations Charter.

This false moral equivalence only encourages terrorists to persist in their unlawful actions against civilians. The United States has it exactly right by placing the blame on Hamas, while urging Israel to do everything possible to minimize civilian casualties.

[6] Intelligence and Terrorism Information Center at the Israel Intelligence Heritage & Commemoration Center (IICC), "Summary of rocket fire and mortar shelling in 2008," Jan. 1, 2009, < http://www.terrorism-info.org.il/malam_multimedia/English/eng_n/pdf/ipc_e007.pdf>.

Chapter 2
Israel's Policy is Perfectly 'Proportionate'

After several days of air attacks, Israel was accused of taking disproportionate action to prevent Hamas rockets from hitting civilian targets in Israel. I submitted the following article to the Wall Street Journal *on that issue. It was published on January 2, 2009.*

Hamas are the real war criminals in this conflict.

Israel's actions in Gaza are justified under international law, and Israel should be commended for its self-defense against terrorism. Article 51 of the United Nations Charter reserves to every nation the right to engage in self-defense against armed attacks. The only limitation international law places on a democracy is that its actions must satisfy the principle of proportionality.

Since Israel ended its occupation of Gaza, Hamas has fired thousands of rockets designed to kill civilians into southern Israel. The residents of Sderot—which have borne the brunt of the attacks—have approximately 15 seconds from launch time to run into a shelter. Although deliberately targeting civilians is a war crime, terrorists firing at Sderot are so proud of their actions that they sign their weapons.

When Barack Obama visited Sderot this summer and saw the remnants of these rockets, he reacted by saying that if his two daughters were exposed to rocket attacks in their home, he would do everything in his power to stop such attacks. He understands how the terrorists exploit the morality of democracies.

In a recent incident related to me by the former head of the Israeli air force, Israeli intelligence learned that a family's house in Gaza was being used to manufacture rockets. The Israeli military gave the residents 30 minutes to leave. Instead, the owner called Hamas, which sent mothers carrying babies to the house.

Hamas knew that Israel would never knowingly fire at a home with civilians in it. They also knew that if Israeli authorities did not learn there were civilians in the house and fired on it, Hamas would win a public relations victory by displaying the dead. Israel held its fire. The Hamas rockets that were protected by the human shields were then used against Israeli civilians.

These despicable tactics—targeting Israeli civilians while hiding behind Palestinian civilians—can only work against moral democracies that care deeply about minimizing civilian casualties.

Candidate Obama inspects Hamas rocket shells in Sderot.

The Hamas tactic would not have worked against the Russians in Chechnya. When the Russians were fired upon, they fired against civilians without hesitation, killing thousands (with little international protest). Nor would it work in Darfur, where Janjaweed militias have killed thousands of civilians and displaced 2.5 million in order to get the rebels who were hiding among them. Certain tactics work only against moral enemies who care deeply about minimizing civilian casualties.

The claim that Israel has violated the principle of proportionality—by killing more Hamas terrorists than the number of Israeli civilians killed by Hamas rockets—is absurd. First, there is no legal equivalence between the deliberate killing of innocent civilians and the deliberate killings of Hamas combatants. Under the laws of war, any number of combatants can be killed to prevent the killing of even one innocent civilians.

Second, proportionality is not measured by the number of civilians actually killed, but rather by the risk posed by those who are being targeted by the military action. This is illustrated by what happened on Tuesday, when a Hamas rocket hit a kindergarten in Beer Sheva, though no students were there at the time. Under international law, Israel is not required to allow Hamas to play Russian roulette with its children's lives. It may take whatever military action it reasonably believes is necessary to stop the rockets from being fired *before* they kill the civilians Hamas is targeting with its thousands of anti-personnel rockets.

While Israel installs warning systems and builds shelters, Hamas refuses to do so, precisely because it wants to maximize the number of Palestinian civilians inadvertently killed by Israel's military actions. Hamas knows from experience that even a small number of innocent Palestinian civilians killed inadvertently will result in bitter condemnation of Israel by many in the international community.

Israel understands this as well. It goes to enormous lengths to reduce the number of civilian casualties—even to the point of foregoing legitimate targets that are too close to civilians.

Until the world recognizes that Hamas is committing three war crimes—targeting Israeli civilians, using Palestinian civilians as human shields, and seeking the destruction of a member state of the United Nations—and that Israel is acting in self-defense and out of military necessity, the conflict will continue.

Moral Clarity

Candidate Barack Obama at Sderot: I don't think any country would find it acceptable to have missiles raining down on the heads of their citizens.

The first job of any nation state is to protect its citizens. And so I can assure you that if—I don't even care if I was a politician. If somebody was sending rockets into my house where my two daughters sleep at night, I'm going to do everything in my power to stop that. And I would expect Israelis to do the same thing.

In terms of negotiations with Hamas, it is very hard to negotiate with a group that is not representative of a nation state, does not recognize your right to exist, has consistently used terror as a weapon, and is deeply influenced by other countries. I think that Hamas leadership will have to make a decision at some point as to whether it is a serious political party seeking to represent the aspirations of the Palestinian people. And, as a consequence, willing to recognize Israel's right to exist and renounce violence as a tool to achieve its aims. Or whether it wants to continue to operate as a terrorist organization. Until that point, it's hard for Israel, I think, to negotiate with a country that—or with a group that doesn't recognize Israel's right to exist as a country.

Chapter 3
Dershowitz-Zogby Debate CNN: Part I

On January 3, Wolf Blitzer invited me to appear on the Larry King Show (which he was hosting) to debate James Zogby about the ongoing conflict. Here is that debate:

CNN LARRY KING LIVE

Israeli Troops Grind into Gaza; Deadly Conflict Threatens Humanitarian Crisis

Aired January 3, 2009–21:00 ET

Blitzer: So what should the United States be doing right now?

Joining us, two special quests, the Harvard law professor, Alan Dershowitz. His new book is entitled *The Case Against Israel's Enemies.* Its publisher is Wiley.

Also joining us here in Washington is James Zogby, the president of the Arab-American Institute.

Jim, what should the outgoing Bush administration and the incoming Obama administration be doing right now?

James Zogby, President, Arab-Amerian Institute: Most certainly, what the Bush administration should do is learn the lessons of the past. Their own past, actually. A cease-fire immediately is what's in order. This is going nowhere, but actually bringing everybody into hell. It's going to be Lebanon all over again. Moderates are going to be weakened, extremists strengthened. Hamas will be hurt, but extremism in the region will be aided by this venture.

And, you know, the Israelis are doing it in order to win an election, but at what cost. The cost will be an enormous setback for them in the broader region.

If America were a friend of Israel, it would call for an end now. What you do in the long term is, you've got to end the occupation. This is getting us nowhere, getting Israel in deeper and hurting the Palestinians more.

Blitzer: Alan Dershowitz, you're looking at the live pictures from Gaza. You see the plumes of smoke coming up. This fighting clearly escalating, intensifying even as we speak. What should the outgoing Bush administration and the incoming Obama administration be doing?

Alan Dershowitz, Law Professor, Harvard University: It should recognize that Hamas and other terrorist groups have created a terrible dilemma for democracies by firing rockets at citizens, one million of them. One recently hit a kindergarten. Could have killed 50 or 60 young Israeli children. And then hiding behind civilians and having the rockets come from civilians, they put democracy to a terrible choice. Either do nothing and let your own civilians be killed, which no democracy could do, or respond and be accused of disproportionality, because whenever you respond effectively to that kind of tactic, it will involve civilian deaths.

Look, let's think of an analogy. If a bank robber holds a hostage, and starts shooting from behind the hostage, and a policeman, in an effort to stop the shooting by the bank robber, shoots and kills the hostage, under the law of every country, it's the bank robber who's guilty of murder, not the policeman. That's what's going on.

Blitzer: Hold on...

Dershowitz: Unless you learn that lesson, this tactic will persist.

Blitzer: I want to point out the live pictures you're seeing. Take a look at that. You're seeing these live pictures coming in from Gaza right now. We don't know what's causing those plumes of smoke to go up there, but it clearly looks like this fighting is intensifying.

Jim Zogby, go ahead.

Zogby: Alan, this isn't a bank robbery. The reality here, Wolf, is these bombs are falling on Gaza, terrorizing young children in Gaza. And the fact is that the trauma that this creates will play itself out in the long term, as it has been playing itself out since this all began, when the occupation started some 40-something years ago. We have to find a way to get out of this hole.

And what Alan proposes and what the Israeli government is doing has no end game. The fact here is that there are pathologies playing out on both sides. What they need is adult supervision. And the United States has been absent.

So you ask what needs to be done. Alan says nothing.

Dershowitz: No, I don't say nothing.

Zogby: Let the Israelis play it out. I say, no, stop it now. And begin to find, as the Bush administration has not done, a political way out of this.

We did have an opportunity, some few years ago, when the Saudi Arabians organized and helped create a Mecca accord. Israel didn't honor it. And the U.S. wouldn't support it.

Blitzer: Alan Dershowitz, you said the U.S. should be doing something. What should the U.S. be doing?

Dershowitz: They should be doing what they did under Bill Clinton, and that is offer the Palestinians a two-state solution. Hamas has repeatedly rejected that. The problem is you can't try to start with the Saudi initiatives or any of the other initiatives when Hamas, which controls Gaza, simply won't recognize Israel's right to exist.

Hamas is not concerned about the occupation since '67. Jim and I agree that the occupation should be ended. They believe all of Israel is occupied. They talk about a 60-year occupation, not a 41-year occupation.

So Israel has to, in order to make peace, make sure that Hamas is not in control of the Gaza and can't scuttle any peace effort by rockets. If it can defeat and destroy Hamas in the Gaza, that will be a very important step toward peace. It could then make peace with the Palestinian [Authority].

Blitzer: These are live pictures you're seeing right now from Gaza. You can see on the left part of your screen, that looks like a mosque with a minaret going up there.

BREAKING NEWS
ISRAEL'S GROUND ATTACK

CRISIS
MIDDLE EAST

LIVE
CNN

IDF: 30 rockets launched from Gaza into Israel Sunday

Jim Zogby, as you see these pictures, and these are incredible, what goes through your mind?

Zogby: I've been there. I've been to Jabalya. I've been to Gaza City.

Blitzer: Before the refugee camps?

Zogby: I've been to Gaza City. It is the most densely populated place on earth. What, with Ron Brown, he said there was no place poorer. He called it worse than Soweto.

The fact is you have 1.5 million people, more than half little children, playing, for the most, part in open sewage, because it is desperately poor. And Israel provided no infrastructure. Now they're being terrorized this way.

We have learned from the past that wars of this sort do not defeat the enemy. What they end up doing is creating a greater sense of solidarity.

So what is going to happen here is what happened when Alan and I debated in 2006. And he said they were going to eliminate Hezbollah. Hamas and the extremist currents will be strengthened. People will be angry. Every one of those people who died, their family, and they will never forgive Israel or the United States for this.

The point is that Israel doesn't understand. There's no end game here. And so their pathologies are no different than the pathologies of the other side. They need to be stopped and restrained. And America has to help.

Blitzer: Alan Dershowitz, when you see these pictures, what goes through your mind?

Dershowitz: I've been there too. I've been to Sderot. I was there one night when a rocket hit.

Blitzer: Sderot is in southern Israel.

Dershowitz: Right. I saw the thousands of rockets. Barack Obama went there as well. And he said what I said, and that is, if my children were being exposed to rocket fire every night, I would understand what Israel has to do to stop it.

My question to your audience, and even to Jim, is what would you do if rockets were raining down on you? You would have to put an end to it. If a cease-fire will put an end to it, fine. If a political resolution puts an end to it, fine. When you have Hamas, that broke the cease-fire, that said we will not respect the cease-fire, that will use a temporary cease-fire to simply rearm, you have to ask yourself what would you do.

Zogby: Alan, I'm not going to shill for Hamas. They are wrong and they have been wrong. Even before this all began they've been wrong. But the Israeli government is not right either. And America has to help...

Dershowitz: What should Israel do?

Zogby: Unfortunately, Israel apparently can't help itself because it keeps making the wrong choices.

Dershowitz: What would you do?

Zogby: I would ask America to help provide restraint and to help create a condition for Israel and the Palestinians.

Dershowitz: I agree.

Blitzer: Guys, we have to wrap it up right there. But our coverage will continue.

Jim Zogby, Alan Dershowitz, thanks to both of you.

Chapter 4
Dershowitz-Zogby Debate CNN: Part II

The debate with Zogby proved so popular, that Larry King invited us back the next day to continue the debate. Here is the second installment of my debate with James Zogby:

CNN LARRY KING LIVE

Aired January 4, 2009–21:00 ET

King: Joining us now in Miami, Alan Dershowitz, professor of Harvard Law School, best-selling author and his latest book is *The Case Against Israel's Enemies.* In Washington, James Zogby, president of the Arab American institute.

Now we all know what's been going on. We've heard the previous segment.

Alan, why is Israel right?

Dershowitz: Israel is right because no democracy is required to play Russian roulette with the lives of its children. 6,000 missiles have hit in Israel. They've hit kindergartens, they've hit schools.

Fortunately, Israel has built shelters and they've had only a few dozen casualties. But it's only a matter of time until a rocket hits a kindergarten with 40 or 50 kids in it.

Proportionality doesn't require a nation to sit back and accept these kinds of missiles. The fact that civilians are being killed is completely the fault of Hamas for hiding behind civilians.

They are committing a triple war crime by targeting Israeli civilians, by using their own civilians as human shields, and by calling for the destruction of a member state of the United Nations.

King: James, there's no question there, is there, that Hamas started this?

James Zogby, President, Arab American Institute: Well, listen, the fact is that there has been an ongoing conflict between the Palestinians and the Israelis over that border in Gaza since the beginning of the occupation in 1967.

Dershowitz: Over the border in Gaza? There's no dispute about the border.

Zogby: Israel withdrew, as they said, in 2005 but continued to maintain almost complete closure over Gaza, making it impossible for decent human life to take place. Unemployment among youth, 80 percent, unemployment in the entire country, 70 percent. 40—50 percent among the adult population. But the poverty level is crushing and the fact here is that even when the cease-fire was winding down, Israel chose that moment to make a provocation by crossing into the border on an assault against Hamas fighters.

Hamas Combatants with missile launcher, surrounded by civilians.

Now there is no side here that's right. I am not going to be a defender of Hamas's provocative behavior. But neither should Alan be defending what Israel has done or is doing now.

The fact is, both sides are playing out pathologies and there's no adult supervision. I fault the United States...

King: Alan?

Zogby: ... for not helping to unwind the situation years ago and certainly for not providing restraint.

Now Alan is making the same...

King: Alan...

Zogby: ... arguments that he made today that he made in 2006 when the Lebanon travesty was taking place. The outcome would be the same.

King: Now that does...

Zogby: Nothing good will come of this.

King: Alan, does James—Alan, does James have a point?

Dershowitz: No, he doesn't have a point, unfortunately.

King: No point?

Dershowitz: The international border has been recognized. Israel pulled back completely and there's no dispute about the border at all. And in fact, the reason why Hamas is suffering from poverty is because all the money they've gotten has been spent on buying missiles, on digging tunnels. The corruption has denied the people of Palestine hospital care and medical care.

They've made a decision to destroy their own people. And don't come crying to the international community that there is a humanitarian crisis, when the Hamas government has caused the humanitarian crisis. Under Article 51 Israel is entitled to respond by saying we are going to win this war. We're going to demand an unconditional surrender the way Great Britain did when Germany fired missiles at it and the way the United States did when Pearl Harbor was attacked.

Zogby: Way, the way to unwind extremism and the way, ultimately, to isolate and defeat Hamas is to provide an opportunity for the Palestinians to feel hope. They feel no hope and Israel has given them no opportunity to feel hope.

King: James Zogby, getting down to the crux of it, how does this end? Logically, how does this end?

Zogby: Well, when Israel has entered now into Gaza with a massive ground force, one sees actually a difficulty in how it ends. The fact is that it will be much more difficult to leave than it was to go in. The casualty rate is simply increasing among civilians.

Alan says because Hamas hides behind civilians, but this is one of the most densely populated places on earth. And unlike any other place on earth, refugees have nowhere to go. They cannot cross a border. There is no border to cross.

Israel controls access…

King: All right.

Zogby: … and egress from everywhere. And, therefore, what is happening here is that the 500, 600, 700, lord knows how many, will die before it's over. Families will hate and fear and be angry for the rest of their lives and then some.

And so there is no good that comes of this.

King: All right. Alan…

Zogby: And there probably will be a cease-fire but with enormous pain, and frankly, the majority of that on the Palestinian side. This is not a good thing.

King: Alan. Alan, how does it end, Alan?

Dershowitz: It ends with Hamas being weakened and hopefully destroyed so that Israel can then sit down with the Palestinians and offer them again what Bill Clinton and what Ehud Barak offered them in 2000 and 2001—a state, the end of the occupation, a divided Jerusalem, a refugee reparations program. Remember, the Palestinians could have had a state in 1938, 1948, 1967, 2001, but they have always wanted to destroy the Jewish state more than they have ever wanted their own state. Now the Palestinians...

Zogby: That's not true, Alan.

Dershowitz: ... people through the PLO claim that they want a two- state solution. And Hamas is standing in the way of it. And the people who are rooting most loudly for the destruction of Hamas in Gaza are the Palestinian authority.

You know, if any member of the Palestinian authority walks into Gaza today, they'll get murdered. Gaza today is a terrorist state.

Zogby: There is no...

Dershowitz: And the best thing that could happen would be the weakening or destruction of Hamas in Gaza.

King: All right. James, why is that wrong?

Dershowitz: And sitting down and creating a two-state solution.

Zogby: Israel was going to destroy the PLO in '82, it didn't. They were going to destroy Hezbollah in—2006, they didn't. They were going to destroy Hamas in 2006, and they didn't. This is not the way you defeat extremism. What it does is it makes the extremist current more—in fact, more virulent than before and creates more supporters.

The weak—the party that will be weakened in all of this, tragically, are the moderates like President Abbas and moderate Arab leaders who are looking weak in the eyes of their own people.

Dershowitz: But, Jim, you are a reasonable guy.

Zogby: Listen, Alan...

Dershowitz: What would you do if you were an Israeli? Would you not—would you not defend your people against rocket attacks? What would you do?

Zogby: If I were an Israeli, I wouldn't be building settlements. I wouldn't have...

Dershowitz: Forget about that. We're talking about Gaza now.

Zogby: And I wouldn't have walls, and I wouldn't, in Gaza, strangle the people of Gaza so that Hamas had the support that it did, the fact is that the fact strangulation and deprivation of the people of Gaza has been going for years now.

Dershowitz: But they would still be firing rockets.

Zogby: And therefore, I ask the question.

Dershowitz: Read their charter.

Zogby: I ask the question, Alan.

Dershowitz: Yes.

Zogby: You say to me what would I do if bombed...

Dershowitz: Yes, what would you do now?

Zogby: I ask you what you would do if you could not feed your family?

If you could not find a job? If you were denied the opportunity to live.

Dershowitz: I would overthrow the government of Hamas and make them feed my people instead of buying rockets and sending them into Israel and throw out the people who were destroying Gaza.

Zogby: And what Israel is doing is not going to help that, and that is the tragedy is that neither side will benefit from this.

Dershowitz: You know what...

Zogby: And that's the tragedy.

Dershowitz: What Barack Obama...

Zogby: We're playing off the same song we have played off in 2006.

Dershowitz: No, that's not true. What Barack Obama said...

Zogby: You did not accomplish anything then and it's not accomplishing anything now.

Dershowitz: Don't say me, it's the Israeli government.

Zogby: You defend it, Alan.

Dershowitz: What Barack—what Barack Obama...

Zogby: You were the counsel.

Dershowitz: What Barack Obama said when he went to Sderot.

King: All right. Guys, I need to get a break.

Dershowitz: ... is true. He should do—he would do anything to stop rocket attacks against his daughters.

PRC Rocket fire into Israeli territory.

King: OK. We'll be back with more. Both these guys like the Beatles, by the way.

(LAUGHTER)

King: Thought I'd throw that in. We'll be right back.

King: Alan Dershowitz, James Zogby. Alan, can the Bush administration, in its waning days, get involved and help solve this?

Dershowitz: Yes, I think they can. What I think they have to do is make it very clear that what Israel is doing is in defense of all democracies that are fighting terrorism. Terrorists have figured out a way of making it difficult for democracies.

That is, by attacking their civilians, hiding behind civilians and then showing the media the dead, quote, "children and women." It makes it very difficult to protect and defend their own citizens. If this works in Gaza, it is coming to a theater near you. It will become the paradigm for attacking democracies all over the world.

And that's why Israel has to be encouraged to put an end to the rocket attacks. And I have asked Jim Zogby a dozen times what would you do now if your people were being attacked? If rockets were hitting your schools? If rockets were hitting your kindergartens?

If Russian roulette was being played with your children? Would you simply sit back and let it happen or would you stop the rockets? And how do you stop the rockets?

King: All right. That is—that's a fair question, Jim. How would you respond?

Zogby: The answer here is that, of course, one has the right to self- defense and the issue, though, is one has to look at how you effectively do that, and you quoted Barack Obama a while ago.

Dershowitz: Right.

Zogby: But Barack Obama also said something else quite interesting when he spoke to Jewish leadership in Cleveland in 2008. He said, if the only way we can find a way to make peace for Israel, if you think the only way, he said to the Jewish leadership, is that we have to help Israel destroy all of its enemies and never talk to them, we're not going to move—get progress going forward on that.

Dershowitz: I agree on that.

Zogby: The fact here is that all Israel has done has been to strangle Gaza and to retaliate and constantly strike against the Palestinian people. It has not offered them any opening toward peace.

You say they want to make peace. Wait, Alan. You say they want to make peace in the West Bank with the Palestinian leadership there.

Dershowitz: Right.

Zogby: But what they have done is humiliate them with settlements and with roadblocks and with the wall that continues to snake into the territories, taking more land all the time

Dershowitz: Ending that will not stop terrorism.

Zogby: The fact is, is that if you want to make peace and you want to stop the rockets, you then find a way to give people hope, to isolate extremists and give Palestinians a sense that the future can be brighter than today.

Dershowitz: I agree with that.

Zogby: I want that. I want it for the Israelis and the Palestinian people.

Dershowitz: Jim...

Zogby: But what Israel is doing is not helping to move the ball forward now, before and I fear into the future, because no one is helping them do the right thing.

Dershowitz: Jim...

Zogby: Neither Bush nor you, in defending their action, is helping them make the right choices for peace.

Dershowitz: When Prince Bandar, who was the representative of Saudi Arabia, went to the Camp David meeting and said to Arafat, you are committing a crime against the Palestinian people by rejecting the offer of statehood, 98 percent of the West Bank, full, complete statehood in Gaza, capital in Jerusalem and reparations, $35 billion.

And Arafat walked away from statehood, that was the tragedy that led to this all.

Zogby: I know, but that's not what happened at Camp David.

Dershowitz: I'm quoting Dennis Ross.

Zogby: Yes.

Dershowitz: That's what your opinion is but let me tell you, the people who were there know what happened.

Zogby: I have spoken to the people who were including American negotiators.

Dershowitz: The Palestinians turned down statehood.

Zogby: Read Rob Malley and you'll—get a very different narrative of what happened at Camp David.

Dershowitz: Well, that's why Rob Malley is not currently advising the government. When Barack Obama becomes the president, he will understand how to do what Bill Clinton tried to do and Ehud Barak have tried to do and the Palestinian people will have a chance to get statehood again but only if Hamas is weakened.

King: All right.

Zogby: You're a great lawyer for guilty clients, Alan. It doesn't work, though, in this case.

Dershowitz: That's a cheap shot.

Zogby: Well, I'm sorry, but you've made cheap shots all night.

Dershowitz: That's a cheap shot.

Zogby: Sorry about that.

King: Jim, the one point he asked, you didn't answer.

Zogby: Right.

King: If you were being attacked, would you attack back?

Zogby: Retaliate, you have the right to defend your own citizens.

King: Would you retaliate?

Zogby: But you also cannot take continued, provocative actions that put your citizens at risk and expect anything other than this. Israel has set itself up. Hamas has set itself up.

That's why I said, Larry, we have two pathologies playing out with no adult supervision.

Dershowitz: Now you're blaming the victims.

Zogby: I'm blaming both sides because have become victims of each other. And both...

King: Thank you both very much.

Zogby: ... are making more victims every single day.

King: We'll have you on again.

(CROSSTALK)

King: Great having you both with us.

Chapter 5
The CNN Strategy

During my two debates with James Zogby, CNN flashed pictures of women, children and other civilians who had been killed during the Israeli attacks. They juxtaposed these gruesome pictures over my statements about Israel's legitimate right to defend itself and Hamas's criminal use of human shields. The next day I received many letters from people complaining about the juxtaposition arguing that it was difficult to process my rational words while watching these emotional images. That led me to publish an article describing what Hamas itself calls "The CNN strategy." This article appeared in The National Post *in Canada on January 7, 2009.*

As Israel persists in its military efforts—by ground, air and sea—to protect its citizens from deadly Hamas rockets, and as protests against Israel increase around the world, the success of the abominable Hamas double war crime strategy becomes evident. The strategy is as simple as it is cynical: Provoke Israel by playing Russian roulette with its children, firing rockets at kindergartens, playgrounds and hospitals; hide behind its own civilians when firing at Israeli civilians; refuse to build bunkers for its own civilians; have TV cameras ready to transmit every image of dead Palestinians, especially children; exaggerate the number of civilians killed by including as "children" Hamas fighters who are 16 or 17 years old and as "women," female terrorists.

Hamas itself has a name for this. They call it "the CNN strategy" (this is not to criticize CNN or any other objective news source for doing its job; it is to criticize Hamas for exploiting the freedom of press which it forbids in Gaza). The CNN strategy is working because decent people all over the world are naturally sickened by images of dead and injured children. When they see such images repeatedly flashed across TV screens, they tend to react emotionally. Rather than asking why these children are dying and who is to blame for putting them in harm's way, average viewers, regardless of their political or ideological perspective, want to see the killing stopped. They blame those whose weapons directly caused the deaths, rather than those who provoked the violence by deliberately targeting civilians.

They forget the usual rules of morality and law. The use of human shields, in the way Hamas uses the civilian population of Gaza, is a war crime—as is its firing of rockets at Israeli civilians. Every human shield that is killed by Israeli self-defence measures is the responsibility of Hamas, but you wouldn't know that from watching the media coverage.

The CNN strategy seems to work better, at least in some parts of the world, against Israel than it would against other nations. There is much more protest—and fury—directed against Israel when it inadvertently kills approximately 100 civilians in a just war of self-defence, than against Arab and Muslim nations and groups that deliberately kill far more civilians for no legitimate reason.

It isn't the nature of the victims, since more Arabs and Muslim civilians are killed every day in Africa and the Middle East by Arab and Muslim governments and groups with little or no protests. (For example, on the first day of Israel's ground attack, approximately 30 Palestinians, almost all Hamas combatants, were killed. On the same day an Islamic suicide bomber blew herself up in a mosque in Iraq, killing 40 innocent Muslims. No protests. Little media coverage.)

It isn't the nature of the killings, since Israel goes to extraordinary lengths to avoid killing civilians—if for no other reason than that it hurts its cause—while Hamas does everything in its power to force Israel to kill Palestinian civilians by firing its missiles from densely populated civilian areas and refusing to build shelters for its civilians.

It isn't the nature of the conflict, either, because Israel is fighting a limited war of self-defense designed to protect its own civilians from rocket attacks, while most of those killed by Arabs and Muslims are killed in genocidal and tribal warfare with no legitimate aim.

The world simply doesn't seem to care when Arabs and Muslims kill large numbers of other Arabs and Muslims, but a qualitatively different standard applies when the Jewish state kills even a relatively small number of Muslims and Arabs in a war of self-defense.

The international community doesn't even seem to care when Palestinian children are killed by rocket fire—unless it is from Israeli rockets. The day before the recent outbreak, Hamas fired an anti-personnel rocket at Israeli civilians, but the rocket fell short of its target and killed two Palestinian girls. Yet there was virtually no coverage and absolutely no protests against these "collateral" civilian deaths. Hamas refused to allow TV cameras to show these dead Palestinian children.

Nor have there been protests against the cold-blooded murders by Hamas and its supporters of dozens of Palestinian civilians who allegedly "collaborated" with Israel. Indeed, Hamas and Fatah have killed far more Palestinian civilians over the past several years than have the Israelis, but you wouldn't know that from the media, the United Nations or protesters who focus selectively on only those deaths caused by Israeli military actions.

The protesters who filled the streets of London, Paris and San Francisco were nowhere to be seen when hundreds of Jewish children were murdered by Palestinian terrorists over the years.[7]

Moreover, the number of civilians killed by Israel is almost always exaggerated. First, it is widely assumed that if a victim is a "child" or a "woman," he or she is necessarily a civilian. Consider the following report in Thursday's *New York Times:* "Hospital officials in Gaza said that of the more than 390 people killed by Israeli fighter planes since Saturday, 38 were children and 25 women." Some of these children and women were certainly civilians, but others were equally certainly combatants.

Hamas often uses 14-, 15-, 16-and 17-year-olds, as well as women, as terrorists. Israel is entitled under international law to treat these "children" and women as the combatants they have become. Hamas cannot, out of one side of its mouth, boast that it recruits children and women to become terrorists, and then, out of the other side of its mouth, complain when Israel takes it at its word. The media should look closely and critically at the number of claimed civilian victims before accepting self-serving and self-contradictory exaggerations.

By any objective count, the number of genuinely innocent civilians killed by the Israeli Air Force in Gaza is lower than the collateral deaths caused by any nation in a comparable situation. Hamas does everything in its power to provoke Israel into killing as many Palestinian civilians as possible, in order to generate condemnation against the Jewish state. It has gone so far as firing rockets from Palestinian schoolyards and hiding its terrorists in Palestinian maternity wards.

The reality is that the elected and de facto government of Gaza has declared war against Israel. Under Article 51 of the United Nations Charter, it has committed an "armed attack" against the Jewish state. The Hamas charter calls for Israel's total destruction. Under international law, Israel is entitled to take whatever military action is necessary to repel that attack and stop the rockets.

It must seek to minimize civilian deaths consistent with the legitimate military goal, and it is doing precisely that, despite Hamas's efforts to maximize civilian deaths on both sides.

---

[7] Israel Ministry of Foreign Affairs, "Victims of Palestinian Violence and Terrorism since September 2000," <http://www.mfa.gov.il/MFA/Terrorism-+Obstacle+to+Peace/Palestinian+terror+since+2000/Victims+of+Palestinian+Violence+and+Terrorism+sinc.htm>, accessed Feb. 20, 2009.

Chapter 6
Hamas's Dead Baby Strategy

After watching "the CNN strategy" operate for several days, I decided that there was really a more appropriate term for Hamas's strategy. Gruesome as it sounds, the more apt term is "Hamas's Dead Baby Strategy." I wrote an article on that subject that was published by The Washington Times *on January 16, 2009.*

Cynical ploy must be exposed and rejected

The Hamas "dead baby" strategy—to cause as many civilian casualties as possible by firing its deadly rockets from schools and densely populated areas—is producing understandable outrage around the world. What is not understandable is why the outrage is directed against Israel, which is a victim of this strategy, rather than against Hamas, which is its perpetrator. Hamas knew exactly what it was doing when it fired more than 6,000 rockets at Israeli kindergartens, elementary schools and playgrounds from behind its own children. It was playing Russian roulette with the lives of Israeli children in order to provoke a defensive response from Israel.

Hamas knew that Israel, like any democracy, would have to take whatever military action was necessary to stop the rockets. As Barack Obama put it when he visited Sderot, a town that had been victimized by more than 1,000 rockets and several deaths: "If somebody was sending rockets into my house where my two daughters sleep at night, I'm going to do everything in my power to stop that. And I would expect Israelis to do the same thing." Hamas also knew that Israel could not stop the rockets aimed at its children without accidentally killing some Palestinian children because Hamas was using Palestinian children as human shields for its rockets. Despite its best efforts to avoid killing civilians - Israel gains nothing from such "collateral damage" and loses much—Israeli missiles have killed dozens of innocent children who were deliberately placed in harm's way by Hamas terrorists.

Hamas also knew that the media would show the dead Palestinian children around the world and cause outrage to be directed against Israel for causing their deaths. Indeed, it had its camera crews out and ready to film and transmit every gruesome image of every dead Palestinian child.

The media, of course, serves as Hamas's facilitator. I am not suggesting that the media not show these horrible images, but rather that they should present them with a critical perspective, indicating the actual cause and the real culprit—namely Hamas and its cynical double war crime strategy of targeting Israeli children and hiding behind Palestinian children.

The international community—most especially the United Nations, which has done nothing about genocides committed by Muslims—is accusing Israel of "war crimes" for defending its civilians against Hamas war crimes. This too is part of the Hamas strategy which the United Nations facilitates.

If the media and the international community continue to play into the dirty hands of Hamas terrorists, its terrorism will continue and spread. Why not? It's a win-win strategy for terrorists and a lose-lose strategy for democracies.

> **"If somebody was sending rockets into my house where my two daughters sleep at night, I'm going to do everything in my power to stop that. And I would expect Israelis to do the same thing."**
>
> — President Barack Obama

THE HAMAS MISSILE DEFENSE SHIELD

Hamas knows that by attacking Israeli civilians, they can secure one of two results: Israel will do nothing and Hamas will succeed in killing Israeli children; or Israel will respond and inevitably kill some Palestinian children, thereby provoking the ire of the media, the international community and ultimately decent people all around the world who are revolted by the cynically manipulated images of dead children.

The Hamas strategy may now be spreading to Lebanon where twice in several days, rockets have targeted Israeli civilian areas. Hezbollah, which denies responsibility for these rockets, actually originated this strategy in the summer of 2006, when it provoked Israel into trying to defend its citizens and its kidnapped soldiers. Other nations in the world are susceptible to similar strategies, as the United States learned, when it went after the Taliban and Al Qaeda in Afghanistan and discovered that they too use civilians as human shields.

Unless this "dead baby" strategy is exposed and rejected in the marketplace of morality, it's coming to a theater (or school or hospital) near you.

Chapter 7
Hamas's War Crimes

As the Israel Defense Forces continued to disable rocket launchers, ammunition tunnels and Hamas terrorists, the United Nations called for a cease fire, despite the continuation of Hamas rocket launchings. On January 10, 2009, I published the following in the Los Angeles Times.

A temporary cease-fire in Gaza that simply allows Hamas to obtain more lethal weapons will assure a repetition of Hamas's win-win tactic of firing rockets at Israeli civilians while using Palestinian civilians as human shields.

The best example of Hamas's double war crime tactic was Tuesday, when it succeeded in sending a rocket to a town less than 20 miles south of Tel Aviv and injuring a child. At the same time, it provoked Israel to attack a United Nations school from which Hamas was launching its rockets. Residents of the neighborhood said two Hamas fighters were in the area at the time, and the Israeli military said they had been killed, according to the *New York Times*.

The Hamas tactic of firing rockets from schools, hospitals and mosques dates back to 2005, when Israel ended its occupation of Gaza. Several months ago, the head of the Israeli air force showed me a videotape (now available on YouTube) of a Hamas terrorist deliberately moving his rocket launcher to the front of a U.N. school, firing a rocket and then running away, no doubt hoping that Israel would then respond by attacking the rocket launcher and thus killing Palestinian children in the school.

This is the Hamas dual strategy: to kill and injure as many Israeli civilians as possible by firing rockets indiscriminately at Israeli civilian targets, and to provoke Israel to kill as many Palestinian civilians as possible to garner world sympathy.

Lest there be any doubt about this, recall the recent case of Nizar Rayan, the Hamas terrorist and commander killed in Gaza by an Israeli missile strike Jan. 1. Israeli authorities had warned him that he was a legitimate military target, as was his home, which was a storage site for rockets. This is the same man who in 2001 sent one of his sons on a suicide mission to blow himself up at a Jewish settlement in Gaza. Rayan had the option of moving his family to a safe area. Instead, his four wives and children remained with him as human shields and became martyrs as Israel targeted his home for destruction.

Hamas leaders have echoed the mantra of Hassan Nasrallah, the leader of Hezbollah, that "we are going to win because they love life and we love death."

It is difficult to fight an enemy that loves death in a world that loves life. The world tends to think emotionally rather than rationally when it is shown dead women and children who are deliberately placed in harm's way by Hamas. Instead of asking who was really to blame for these civilian deaths, people place responsibility on those who fired the fatal shots.

The international law of war makes it a war crime to use human shields in the way Hamas does. It also makes it a war crime for Hamas to target Israeli civilians with anti-personnel rockets loaded with ball bearings and shrapnel designed to kill as many civilians as possible.

In Lebanon in 2006, Hezbollah used this same tactic in its war with Israel, setting up civilians to be in harm's way of Israeli responses to rocket fire. When Israel accidentally killed civilians, Hezbollah celebrated them as martyrs. Similarly, the Hamas leadership quietly celebrates the deaths they provoke by causing Israel to fire at its rocket launchers, treating the dead Palestinian civilians as martyrs. *The New York Times* reported Friday that a wounded fighter was smiling at the suffering of civilians, saying "they should be happy" because they "lost their loved ones as martyrs."

The best proof of Hamas's media strategy of manipulating sympathy is the way it dealt with a rocket it fired the day before Israel's airstrikes began. The rocket fell short of its target in Israel and landed in Gaza, killing two young Palestinian girls. Hamas, which exercises total control of Gaza, censored any video coverage of those deaths. Although there were print reports, no one saw pictures of these two dead Palestinian children because they were killed by Palestinian rockets rather than by Israeli rockets. Hamas knows that pictures are more powerful than words. That is probably why Israel has—mistakenly in my view—kept foreign journalists from entering the war zone.

Israel must continue to try to stop the Hamas rockets that endanger more than a million Israeli civilians. It also must continue to do everything in its power to avoid Palestinian civilian casualties, not only because that is the right thing to do but because every Palestinian death plays into the hands of Hamas's leaders.

A good day for Hamas is when one of its rockets kills Israeli civilians and provokes Israel into attacking rocket launchers placed by Hamas near Palestinian civilians, some of whom are accidentally killed in the crossfire.

A bad day for Hamas is a day in which its rockets fail to kill or injure any Israeli civilians and Israel kills no Palestinian civilians. That is what Israel and the world must strive for. Hamas knows that the moment it ends its policy of firing rockets at Israeli civilians from behind the shield of Palestinian civilians, Israel will end its military activities in Gaza. That is precisely the result Hamas does not want to achieve.

Chapter 8
Hamas Provoked Response

On January 12, 2009 I was invited to address a rally in Miami Beach, Florida in support of peace in Gaza. This rally followed a stridently anti-Israel rally in Fort Lauderdale at which participants were videotaped calling for more gas chambers and more crematoria for the Jews. Peace was hardly mentioned at the anti-Israel rally. At the rally in which I participated, peace was mentioned dozens of times. Prayers were offered for peace. Every speaker bemoaned the death of innocent Palestinian civilians. I published my speech as an article in the Miami Herald *on January 16, 2009.*

The war in Gaza is as pure a conflict between good and evil as I have experienced. An anti-Semitic terrorist group whose charter calls for the destruction of Israel and whose leaders incite genocide against the Jewish people are employing a new weapon in a cynical effort to obtain international support for their bigoted aims: their new weapon is the use of civilians as both targets and shields.

The use of civilians as deliberate weapons of warfare is forbidden by international law, yet many in the international community—especially within the UN—are encouraging the use of this insidious weapon either by directly supporting the criminals who are employing it, or by declaring a moral equivalence between terrorists who deliberately target civilians and democracies that inadvertently kill civilians who were deliberately placed in harm's way by the terrorists.

What Hamas is doing should be evident to anyone with an objective eye and common sense. They are provoking Israel to take military action against those terrorists who are raining deadly rockets at a million Israeli civilians and playing Russian roulette with the lives of Israeli children. They know that any democracy in the world would have to respond militarily to these armed attacks against its civilians. Because Hamas deliberately fires its rockets from densely populated areas—including from schools, mosques and private homes—they knew that any Israeli military action will cause Palestinian civilian casualties.

For Hamas this creates a win-win situation: if Israel does nothing and allows the rockets to continue to be fired at Israeli civilians, Hamas wins. It's only a matter of time and luck before a Hamas rocket hits a school filled with children and Hamas celebrates its success. If, on the other hand, Israel takes military action to stop the rockets, they are sure to kill some Palestinian children. Hamas had made sure of that by firing its rockets from areas where children are going to be in proximity to Israeli military actions. Hamas stands ready to exploit every civilian death by having its video cameras and reporters ready to record and transmit emotional images of every dead Palestinian child or woman.

It is almost as if Hamas were literally loading Palestinian children into cannons, attaching explosives to their bodies, and firing them as ammunition at Israeli civilians. Wait! Hamas has actually done just that. They have sent children unknowingly carrying explosives into Israel intending to detonate them as human bombs by remote control. They have recruited 13 and 14 year old boys [8] as well as pregnant women as suicide bombers.[9]

What is required in the face of such unmitigated evil is moral clarity and it is precisely that clarity that is missing from the current debate. It is imperative that President elect Obama and his foreign policy team bring a sense of moral clarity to this conflict if they are to have any chance of resolving it in a just and enduring manner.

As an aid to moral clarity, consider the following three analogous situations. An armed bank robber kills several tellers and takes a customer hostage; hiding behind his human shield the robber continues to kill civilians; a police officer, trying to prevent further killings, shoots at the murderer but accidentally kills the hostage. Who is guilty of murder? Not the policeman who fired the fatal shot but the bank robber who fired from behind the human shield. The international law of war, likewise, makes it a war crime to use human shields in the way Hamas does. It also makes it a war crime for Hamas to target Israeli civilians with anti-personnel rockets loaded with ball bearings and shrapnel designed to kill as many civilians as possible.

A second analogy, closer to the Gaza situation, is to other nations that have been attacked by rockets. When German rockets targeted British cities, Churchill responded by carpet bombing German cities. The United States responded similarly to the attack on Pearl Harbor. When terrorists attacked us on 9/11, we sent troops to Afghanistan to destroy the Taliban and Al Qaeda. These counterattacks caused many more civilian casualties than have occurred in Gaza.

Finally, ask yourself, as Barack Obama asked himself when he visited Sderot and saw the rockets that had plagued that city for years, "What would you do?" as President-elect.

Obama responded: Whatever it takes to protect our children.

I recently saw a cartoon which brilliantly encapsulated the situation. It showed an Israeli soldier and a Hamas terrorist shooting at each other. The Israeli soldier was standing in front of a baby carriage, protecting the baby. The Hamas terrorist was firing from behind a baby carriage, using the baby as a shield. Sometimes it takes a cartoon to illustrate moral clarity.

---

[8] Justus Reid Weiner, "The Recruitment of Children in Current Palestinian Strategy," Jerusalem Center for Public Affairs, Oct. 1, 2002, <http://www.jcpa.org/brief/brief2-8.htm>.

[9] Reuters, "Pregnant Palestinian planned suicide bomb—Israel," Jun. 13, 2007, <http://www.reuters.com/article/featuredCrisis/idUSL13877653>.

Chapter 9
Dershowitz-Scobbie Debate BBC

On January 14, 2009, the BBC invited me to debate a well-known anti-Israel international law professor about possible war crime prosecutions against Israel. Here is the debate (it can be seen http://news.bbc.co.uk/2/hi/programmes/newsnight/7828296.stm).

Iain Scobbie, Professor of International Law at SOAS (School of Oriental and African Studies and London University) and Harvard law Professor Alan Dershowitz debate if war crimes have been committed during the Gaza conflict.

Commentator: On what grounds in your view could Israel face war crimes indictment?

Scobbie: War crimes indictment. I think that we could perhaps, obviously this requires investigation, but we could see it in relation to attacks which cause disproportionate civilian casualties. One that's been suggested is when 30 people were killed in Zeitun, when a house was shelled. The ICRC has also criticized an attack on a shelter in Jabalya which was there for displaced persons. The ICRC has also said that the Israel Defense Forces have failed to care for and evacuate the wounded, which is in breach of the Geneva Convention.

Commentator: Any of these in your view amount to a war crime?

Dershowitz: This isn't even a close case. What Israel is doing is fighting a far cleaner war than Great Britain fought against the Germans. If these were war crimes, then Winston Churchill would have been hanged at Nuremburg. Franklin Roosevelt, Harry Truman... would have been hanged. The British Prime Minister would have been hanged for what went on in Kenya, the Russians would have been prosecuted by what went on in Chechnya. Israel is being singled out for doing what every democracy would do when rockets are rained down indiscriminately on its citizens, when its enemy terrorists play Russian roulette with the lives of its children. Three rockets recently hit kindergartens. Fortunately nobody was in them because the kindergarten students were not allowed to go to school. No democracy has to accept rockets being rained down on it indiscriminately. So the question I would pose to my distinguished colleague is: what would international law permit a democracy to do in order stop rockets from indiscriminately being fired on its citizens? Does it have to wait until one hits a school with 100 people, then it would act proportionately?

Scobbie: I think one thing that Prof Dershowitz has forgotten that the occupied Palestinian territories are a democracy. Hamas was elected by popular vote which the world then chose to forget. Leaving that to one side, I don't think there is any doubt that under international law, as it stands today, Hiroshima would be a war crime. It was an indiscriminate attack. The same could probably be said of Dresden. Israel has invoked self-defense. Now one of the requirements of self-defense is that it must be proportionate. Now what that essentially means is to some extent it's a head count. You know whether the consequences of the force used cause disproportionate harm in relation to the injury which might be seen in future attacks. Now if we look at what's happening in Gaza we have coming up to 1000 deaths there... 40% of which the UN says are women and children. In relation to the attacks on Israel.

Commentator: In relation to the attacks on Israel, surely Israel has an absolute right to protect its citizens...

Scobbie: It's got a right to protect its citizens but it must be done proportionally and I think what we are seeing now is a disproportionate attack.

Dershowitz: What would be proportionate to an attack that risks the lives of hundreds of people and exposes a million people to rockets every day? Israel would not be allowed to do anything that wasn't necessary to stop the rockets. Israel hasn't even yet succeeded in stopping the rockets. If the rockets stopped and the attacks continued that would be different.

Commentator: Alan Dershowitz, do you accept that the nature of the attack makes it look to a certain extent that there is a kind of mass guilt among the Palestinians for what is happening, rather than, ok, you say that Hamas uses human shields, but the amount of children killed in these attacks is very high proportionately.

Dershowitz: Well, far less than, for example, of the amount of civilians and children killed in Afghanistan and Iraq by the United States and Great Britain.

Scobbie: I honestly don't think that's the point.

Dershowitz: But remember the important point that was made previously. Hamas is the elected government of the Gaza. That is true and Hamas has engaged under Article 51 of the United Nations charter in an armed attack against the state of Israel by rocketing. In fact, 6,000 armed attacks. Israel waited until 5,000 armed attacks before it responded. It is entitled to stop the rockets. If military action is required to stop the rockets, it's entitled to do that. Remember that Hamas is hiding its fighters behind human shields.

Scobbie: Ok, that's an allegation which has yet to be proved, Professor Dershowitz.

Dershowitz: So is the 400 deaths an allegation that hasn't been proved. Believe me I could prove it to you. I've seen the videotape. I have actually with my own eyes seen a videotape of a Hamas rocketer bringing his rocket in front of a UN school, sending the rocket off, then running away, hoping that Israel would respond by attacking the school. I've seen this video.

Commentator: Ok, we are coming to an end and I really have to ask you the reality of this is, Prof Scobbie, is that even if there was sufficient evidence, because Israel is not a signatory to the ICC and because presumably America, unless Barack Obama changes his mind, would not sign on to bringing Israel in front of a war crimes court.

Professor Iain Scobbie

Dershowitz: That's not the reason. Even if Israel were a signatory that would never happen. The ICC would never bring charges against Israel for what the United States has done, what Great Britain has done. Far worse. What France has done. What every democracy has done. Only in England is this regarded as a close question.

Scobbie: We are in a new area as far as international criminal law is concerned with the creation of the ICC. There is a theoretical possibility of a reference to the ICC by the security counsel as the Security Counsel did in relation to Darfur.

Dershowitz: That would mark the end of international law.

Chapter 10
The Phony War Crimes Accusation Against Israel

As the war in Gaza proceeded, anti-Israel academics from around the world, like Professor Scobbie, began to call for war crime trials to be conducted against Israeli political and military officials. At Tel Aviv University, several radical professors called for a fellow professor to be fired, because she served as a lawyer in the Israeli Judge Advocate Corp. during the Gaza War. These actions led me to write an article entitled "The Phony War Crimes Accusation Against Israel," which was published on Huffington Post *on January 22, 2009.*

Every time Israel seeks to defend its civilians against terrorist attacks, it is accused of war crimes by various United Nations agencies, hard left academics and some in the media. It is a totally phony charge concocted as part of Hamas's strategy—supported by many on the hard left—to delegitimate and demonize the Jewish state. Israel is the only democracy in the world ever accused of war crimes when it fights a defensive war to protect its civilians. This is remarkable, especially in light of the fact that Israel has killed far fewer civilians than any other country in the world that has faced comparable threats. In the most recent war in Gaza fewer than a thousand civilians—even by Hamas's skewed count—have been killed.[10] This, despite the fact that no one can now deny that Hamas had employed a deliberate policy of using children, schools, mosques, apartment buildings and other civilian areas as shields from behind which to launch its deadly anti-personnel rockets. The Israeli Air Force has produced unchallengeable video evidence of this Hamas war crime.

Just to take one comparison, consider the recent wars waged by Russia against Chechnya. In these wars Russian troops have killed tens of thousands of Chechnyan civilians, some of them willfully, at close range and in cold blood. Yet those radical academics who scream bloody murder against Israel (particularly in England) have never called for war crime tribunals to be convened against Russia. Nor have they called for war crime charges to be filed against any other of the many countries that routinely kill civilians, not in an effort to stop enemy terrorists, but just because it is part of their policy.

Nor did we see the Nuremburg-type rallies that were directed against Israel when hundreds of thousands of civilians were being murdered in Rwanda, in Darfur and in other parts of the world. These bigoted hate-fests are reserved for Israel.

The accusation of war crimes is nothing more than a tactic selectively invoked by Israel's enemies. Those who cry "war crime" against Israel don't generally care about war crimes, as such. Indeed they often support them when engaged in by country's they like. What these people care about, and all they seem to care about, is Israel. Whatever Israel does is wrong regardless of the fact that so many other countries do worse.

When I raised this concern in a recent debate, my opponent accused me of changing the subject. He said we are talking about Israel now, not Chechnya or Darfur. This reminded me of a famous exchange between Harvard's racist president, Abbott Lawrence Lowell, and the great American judge Learned Hand. Lowell announced that he wanted to reduce the number of Jews at Harvard, because, "Jews cheat." Judge Hand replied that "Christians also cheat." Lowell responded, "You're changing the subject. We are talking about Jews." Well, you can't just talk about Jews. Nor can you just talk about the Jewish state. Any discussion of war crimes must be comparative and contextual. If Russia did not commit war crimes when its soldiers massacred tens of thousands of Chechnyans (not even in a defensive war) then on what basis could Israel be accused of accidentally killing a far fewer number of human shields in an effort to protect its civilians? What are the standards? Why are they not being applied equally? Can human rights endure in the face of such unequal and selective application? These are the questions the international community should be debating, not whether Israel, and Israel alone, violated the norms of that vaguest of notions called "international law" or the "law of war."

If Israel, and Israel alone among democracies fighting defensive wars, were ever to be charged with "war crimes," that would mark the end of international human rights law as a neutral arbitrator of conduct. Any international tribunal that were to charge Israel, having not charged the many nations that have done far worse, will lose any remaining legitimacy among fair-minded people of good will.

If the laws of war, in particular, and international human rights in general, are to endure, they must be applied to nations in order of the seriousness of the violations, not in order of the political unpopularity of the nations. If the law of war were applied in this manner, Israel would be among the last, and certainly not the first, charged.

Chapter 11
Why A Cease Fire Now Will Fail

On January 18, 2009 efforts were begun to institute a cease fire. At the same time rocket attacks began from Lebanon against northern Israel. I wrote an article about the proposed cease fire.

As the rocket attacks against Israel spread to the north, and as Israel seeks an enduring cease-fire that would protect its civilians from the deadly rockets, the international community and media continue to condemn Israel for the military actions it has taken in defense of its citizens. This chorus of entirely predictable, widespread condemnation is the primary reason why no cease-fire will endure. Eliciting condemnation of Israel is the essence of the overall strategy of Israel's enemies to demonize and delegitimize the Jewish state in the eyes of the world.

The strategy goes back to Yasser Arafat. When he turned down the Clinton-Barak offer of statehood in 2000-2001, the international community and the media focused their criticism on what Prince Bandar of Saudi Arabia rightly characterized as Arafat's "crime against the Palestinian people." In order to redirect the criticism against Israel, Arafat ordered an intifada of terrorism that included the suicide bombings of Israeli civilians. When Israel responded with tough measures, much of the world turned against Israel. Calls for divesiture, boycotts and war-crime trials against Israel increased and criticism of Arafat diminished.

A similar strategy was used by Hezbollah in Lebanon. When it attacked northern Israel and kidnapped several of its soldiers, Hezbollah was initially subject to criticism. Hezbollah then began to fire rockets from densely-populated civilian areas, terrorizing northern Israel. When Israel counterattacked, inevitably killing civilians who were being used as human shields, the condemnation shifted to the Jewish state.

Now we see a repeat of this strategy in Gaza. Hamas deliberately broke the cease-fire by firing rockets into southern Israel from densely-populated cities, using the areas around schools and mosques as launching points. Hamas knew that Israel would have to respond—what would any democracy do if their civilians were being rocketed?—and they knew that Palestinian civilians would die in the process. They also knew that the international community and the media would intensify their criticism with every dead Palestinian civilian. That was their goal: to kill and terrorize as many Israeli civilians as possible; to provoke Israel into killing as many Palestinians as possible; and to generate as much international condemnation against Israel as possible.

A just-released report by the Intelligence and Terrorism Information Center in Israel documents the Hamas double war crime strategy of targeting Israeli civilians by firing rockets from schools, mosques and homes and using Palestinian civilians as human shields. The report proves that Hamas

> "makes extensive use of use of Palestinian civilians as human shields. [T]he terrorist organizations constructed a vast military infrastructure in the Gaza Strip, including a large arsenal of rocket and mortar shells used to target the southern Israeli population (in 2001-2008 more than 8,000 rockets and mortar shell were fired into populated Israeli areas). The terrorists' military infrastructure was hidden in and around civilian homes and dispersed to locations scattered around the Gaza Strip...
>
> The calculated, cynical use of the civilian population as human shields in intended... to make it possible for Hamas and the other terrorist organizations to make political-propaganda gains in the battle for hearts and minds by representing Israel as operating against innocent civilians."

For this despicable strategy to work, the international community and media must play its assigned role of uncritically counting and transmitting images of bodies without asking who is to blame for the civilian deaths. Under international, as well as domestic, law those who use human shields are responsible for their predictable deaths, not those who fired the fatal shots.

Those who condemn Israel for its allegedly "disproportionate" response because more Palestinians than Israelis have been killed do not understand that important concept. A democracy is entitled under international law and under Article 51 of the United Nations charter to stop armed attacks against its civilians. Israel is entitled to take whatever military action is necessary to stop the barrage of rockets that has targeted its civilian population, each of which is an "armed attack" under Article 51. It need not stop its military operation until the rocket attacks stop or are stopped permanently. It may not take military actions that are unnecessary to that legitimate military goal, but any military action that is reasonably necessary to stop the armed attacks is proportional, as a matter of law, morality and common sense.

A cease fire without real teeth—including international monitors who can assure that Hamas will not use the lull to rearm and reorganize—would save lives in the short run. But unless the international community and media stop playing into the hands of Israel's enemies by blaming the victims of aggression, the Hamas strategy of firing rockets at Israel's civilians from behind Palestinian civilians will be employed again and again. It is a win-win strategy for terrorists and those who support them.

---

[10] The total number of civilians killed turned out to be closer to 300. See Yaakov Katz, "'World duped by Hamas death count'," Jerusalem Post, Feb. 15, 2009, <http://www.jpost.com/servlet/Satellite?cid=1233304788684&pagen ame=JPost%2FJPArticle%2FShowFull>.

Chapter 12
Will a Cease Fire Work?

On January 18, 2009 Israel unilaterally agreed to a cease fire. Shortly thereafter, Hamas also unilaterally agreed to a cease fire. I published an article in the Sun Sentinel *on January 20, 2009 entitled "Will A Cease Fire Work?"*

Israel's decision to impose a unilateral cease fire—quickly followed by a Hamas cease fire coupled with threats—will save lives in the short run, but it may end up costing even more lives if it is not accompanied by an unequivocal rejection of the Hamas tactic that provoked this war.

Unless Hamas is permanently disarmed and rendered incapable of smuggling more rockets into Gaza, this terrorist group will always have the upper hand. Whenever it chooses, it can once again provoke Israel into retaliating by firing rockets indiscriminately into Israeli civilian areas and again playing Russian roulette with the lives of its children. It can also cause Israel to kill Palestinian children by simply continuing to use civilians as human shields.

Many Israelis today share a view expressed by Golda Meir many years ago when she said to Palestinian terrorists "we can perhaps someday forgive you for killing our children, but we can never forgive you for making us kill your children." That, in a nutshell, is the difference between the morality of Israel and the immorality of Hamas. Israel mourns the death of every child, Palestinian as well as Israeli, whereas Hamas celebrates the death of every child, whether an Israeli killed by one of their rockets or a Palestinian made a martyr by Hamas using him or her as a human shield.

The use of civilians as weapons of war—both offensive and defensive weapons—has been developed to a low science by Hamas and Hezbollah. Yet the international community rarely condemns this despicable, double war crime tactic. It is quick, however, to condemn Israel when it becomes a victim of this win-win tactic for terrorists and lose-lose tactic for democracies. Some have gone so far as to accuse Israel of war crimes. These same bigots were silent when Russia killed tens of thousands of Chechnyan civilians. They don't care about "war crimes." They only use that concept as a weapon against the Jewish state. As long as the international community and the media continue to act as facilitators for Hamas and Hezbollah, these terrorist groups will continue to use their immoral and illegal tactics. And why not? They win and the democracy loses.

This could all change. All that is required is for the international community—the U.N., so-called human rights groups, international lawyers and the media—to put the blame for this tactic squarely where it belongs: on those who use civilians as weapons, by targeting them and by hiding behind them. But dream on! This is about as likely to happen as Hamas recognizing Israel's right to exist and sitting down with the Palestinian Authority to create a Palestinian state pursuant to the two-state solution. Palestinians will finally get a state when their leaders and the majority of Palestinians want their own state more than they want to see the destruction of the Jewish state. Unfortunately, that is not likely to happen in the near future.

The best we can hope for is an interim two-state solution between the Palestinian Authority, which governs the West Bank, and Israel. The West Bank could then be turned into a "West Berlin" as contrasted with Gaza's "East Berlin." A Marshall Plan for a peaceful West Bank might then demonstrate to the citizens of Gaza the peace dividend they could reap from giving up their futile dreams of destroying Israel, voting the Hamas terrorists out of office, and joining with the Palestinian Authority in achieving lasting peace with the Jewish state.

This is a propitious time to explore this option. We have a new administration, with a President who understands Israel's security needs, and has committed himself to protecting Israel from external threats, while at the same time committing himself to seeking a peaceful resolution from the beginning of his term. President-elect Obama, perhaps because of his heritage, is likely to be trusted more than his predecessor by the Arab and Muslim world. It is also a propitious time because Israel has dealt a devastating blow to the Hamas leadership and terrorists, even if it has not completely destroyed them or their capacity to launch rockets. Israel can only make peace from a position of strength, and the Palestinians will only make peace from a position of weakness.

This may also be a propitious time for Israel to reach out to Syria. The Bush Administration discouraged Israel from doing so, whereas the Obama Administration will surely encourage it to try to make peace with that dictatorship. Returning the Golan Heights, even in a demilitarized status, would be extremely risky for Israel. But eliminating Syria from its alliance of evil with Iran holds significant benefits for the Jewish state. Israel too is holding an election and may have a change of administration. Serious peace negotiations will probably have to await the outcome of that election, but preliminary steps can be taken even now.

This is the time for all sides to realize that an imperfect peace, as long as it increases Israel's security, is preferable to a recurrence of Hezbollah and Hamas-initiated warfare.

Chapter 13
Israel, Gaza and International Law

When the war finally ended, I decided to write an article summarizing the legal and moral situation. I published it in the Jerusalem Post *on January 27, 2009. It was entitled "Israel, Gaza and International Law."*

The cease fire on the ground has not ended the war of words against Israel. Indeed, efforts to charge Israel with war crimes and other violations of international law are escalating. The time has come, therefore, for a common sense legal and moral analysis of the events in Gaza and southern Israel.

Let us begin with an argument that is frequently made against Israel. It is pointed out by supporters of Hamas that the official governing authority of Gaza is Hamas, because Hamas won the election. To the extent this is true, however, it is an argument in justification of Israel's actions. If Hamas is the official government of Gaza and if Hamas ordered the firing of more of than 6,000 deadly rockets at Israeli civilians, then it follows that the government of Gaza has engaged in an armed attack against Israel under Article 51 of the United Nations Charter. In other words, the duly elected government of Gaza and the people who elected them have declared war against the government and people of Israel. This should not be surprising, since the Hamas Charter calls for the military destruction of Israel.

Under international law, and under the UN Charter, Israel has the right to respond to these thousands of armed attacks. Indeed every rocket fired into Israel is an armed attack and Israel is entitled to take whatever military actions is deemed reasonably necessary to stop these armed attacks from occurring. If Hamas were merely a small terrorist gang operating from Gaza but without the approval of the government, it would be more difficult to justify a military response that destroyed government buildings and targeted police. Israeli military actions resulted in civilians dying. Precisely how many is hotly disputed: a report by the Italian Newspaper *Corriere Del Sera* disputed Hamas figures and quoted a doctor in Gaza who put the total number of Palestinians killed, including Hamas terrorists, at less than 600.[11] The sad reality is that people who voted for and actively support a terrorist government bear more responsibility for the actions of their government than they would for a gang operating against the wishes of the government. Surely the voters in Germany who elected Hitler bore more responsibility for Nazi atrocities than the people of Iraq did for the atrocities of the dictator Saddam Hussein, who was never fairly elected.

Israel clearly had the right to take whatever military action was necessary to stop the Hamas government from playing Russian roulette with the lives of its children. So far, no

> **"I don't think there has ever been a time in the history of warfare when an army has made more efforts to reduce civilian casualties and deaths of innocent people than the IDF is doing today in Gaza."**
>
> — Colonel Richard Kemp,
> British Military Expert

Hamas Combatants firing from roof of civilian area.

problem under international law. But here's the rub. International law also requires that Israel's actions must not be disproportional to its military aims and it also prohibits the willful targeting of Palestinian civilians.

To make things even more complicated, international law prohibits the use of human shields to protect combatants from lawful military actions taken by those against whom it has waged an armed attack. And there can be absolutely no doubt that it is the official policy of Hamas to use children, women, schools, mosques, hospitals and other civilian institutions and areas as shields to protect its combatants from legitimate Israeli military actions. In addition to the video evidence showing Hamas fighters deliberately placing their rockets adjacent to UN schools, mosques and to residential areas, there are the express statements of officially-elected Hamas leaders both before and during the fighting. Consider the following public statement delivered by a Hamas legislator, transmitted on Hamas television and widely circulated by video. The legislator's name is Fathi Hammad and here is what he said:

> "[The enemies of Allah] do not know that the Palestinian people has developed its [methods] of death and death-seeking. For the Palestinian people, death has become an industry, at which women excel, and so do all the people living on this land. The elderly excel at this, and so do the mujahideen and the children. This is why they have formed human shields of the women, the children, the elderly, and the mujahideen, in order to challenge the Zionist bombing machine. It is as if they were saying to the Zionist enemy: 'We desire death like you desire life.'" (MEMRI, Middle East Research Institute)

There are videos available for all to watch in which Al-Aqsa TV news broadcasts a report showing a crowd of civilians gathered on the roof of a home that was a military target. Indeed those who arranged for these human shields to protect that military target do not shy away from actually using the term "human shield." On another occasion, a Hamas leader, appearing on television demands that "the people of Palestine should gather as one to protect the Jihad warriors' house," calling for these civilians to "die as warriors."

So here is the legal dilemma faced by democracies such as Israel. They have every right under international law to take whatever military actions are necessary to stop the rockets randomly fired at their civilians. Their enemy uses human shields to prevent Israel from destroying the rockets without also killing Palestinian civilians. All the law requires under these circumstances is that Israel take reasonable precaution to minimize enemy civilian deaths in order to prevent the murder of its own civilians. Has Israel taken such precautions? Let retired British colonel Richard Kemp answer that question as he did in a recent BBC interview. He said that there has been "no time in the history of warfare when an army has made more efforts to reduce civilian casualties and the deaths of innocent people than the [Israel Defense forces did in Gaza.]" To accuse Israel of "war crimes" under these circumstances is to distort international law and expose the bias of the accuser.

---

[11] The total number of terrorist combatants killed now appears to be around 750. The number of civilians killed was around 300. See Jerusalem Post, February 15, 2009. These figures are approximations based on the best available information.

Chapter 14
Teleconference with the Israel Project

On January 28, 2009, the Israel Project asked me to participate in a telephonic press conference with media representatives around the world. Here are some excerpts:

Lanny Davis: Hello everyone. I will just provide a couple of introductory comments and then I will first be introducing Professor Dershowitz. There seems to be no dispute that Hamas intentionally launches rockets to kill civilians. They, in fact, publicly boast that the rockets are aimed at Israeli civilians. That is by definition, under any Convention that one wants to look at, a war crime. So the issue of intent is not in dispute as far as I can tell.

Whereas the Israeli defense forces, when they defend themselves from these terrorist rockets, and I'm using the word "terrorist" very specifically, as defined, as intending to kill civilians, the Israeli defense forces if and when—and of course there have been tragic occurrences of the defense forces killing Palestinian civilians—do not do so intentionally, and that distinction is one that I don't hear being made sufficiently in the media.

Moreover, we also know indisputably that Hamas hides behind and uses as shields civilians when they shoot their rockets. We know that they've located their launchers at or near U.N. compounds, and specifically the UNRWA compound where there was a tragic accident by the Israeli defense forces that killed civilian children and teachers in a school compound. We know without any dispute that there were Hamas rocket launchers in the vicinity of that compound yet we had spokespeople from UNRWA accusing Israel of war crimes, or asking at least for an investigation of war crimes, never mentioning that Hamas had located its rocket launchers in the vicinity of that school.

Now I'd like to introduce Professor Dershowitz.

Dershowitz: The first issue that I want to talk about is the tactic that Hamas has perfected and that Hezbollah before it perfected and that is now being used against the United States and Afghanistan as well, and that's the tactic of provoking Israeli responses by playing Russian roulette with the lives of its children. When I was in Sderot, when President Barack Obama was [later] in Sderot, we saw how life becomes unlivable under rocket attacks when a million Israelis are subject to random rocket attacks. Rockets hit civilian areas, they hit schools, they hit kindergartens, recently two hit kindergartens, fortunately, the principals had dismissed [the children] Hamas knows that ultimately a democracy will have to respond to this kind of provocation, indeed that's why they do it. They want Israel to respond and Hamas wants Israel to kill Palestinian babies and women and children and that's why they create human shields.

It's impossible to fight an enemy that wants you to kill his children and women so that he can show the dead bodies to the news media. When you see dead babies and when you see dead women, you often think not with your mind, not with your analytic skills, but with your heart and your gut. Hamas understands that, which brings us to the issue of proportionality. What proportionality means in international law is simply this. When you have a legitimate military target you must do everything to attack the military target and not cause death or injury unrelated to the military target. Now, the military target obviously that Israel is aiming at, are rockets and terrorists who fire the rockets. Indeed, they haven't even yet succeeded; there are still potential sources of rockets and those are all good military targets. And when Hamas put civilian shields, human shields, around the targets and more people die as the result of that, you don't count numbers to assess proportionality, again going back to what Lanny said, you count intention. And the intention of the Israeli defense forces is to minimize civilian casualties. Assume for a moment hypothetically an amoral Israel. Why would an amoral Israel want to kill civilians? They benefit not at all. As one Western diplomat said about Hamas and Hezbollah terrorists, they have understood the arithmetic of death: When they kill a civilian they win and when Israel kills a civilian they win.

Now what they claim is that they had to do it, they had no choice because there was this blockade. Well, you have to look back, as President Carter never does, at the history of the blockade. You know, when Israel left Gaza it left it with greenhouses and with fertile fields and with built-up areas that could easily have been turned into a paradise. There was no blockade at that point. The blockade began obviously when Hamas took over in Gaza, first by winning the election and then by a coup, military coup in Gaza, and started firing rockets at Israel; 6,000 rockets. That's when Israel imposed a small blockade, a relatively minor blockade.

Let me read to you from *The Times:*

"Gazans argue out of necessity. Israel imposed an economic blockade with Hamas's takeover, limiting the flow of goods"—now listen to these words from *The Times*—"limiting the flow of goods - particularly snacks like chocolate and chips, and sodas—and tripling prices."

Yes, there was a blockade. The blockade was designed to do two things. One, to make sure that rockets weren't sent in to be able to attack Israeli children, and second to put pressure on the people of Gaza who were responsible for having elected a Hamas government. But that blockade was a minor one, there was no humanitarian crisis. In fact when Palestinians from Gaza broke through and went to Al Arish in Egypt they immediately returned because they saw life was much better in Gaza than it was in many parts of Egypt. There were paved roads, there was gas, there was electricity, there were cars, unlike in many, many parts of Egypt and many other parts of the Arab world. Then the third phase, of course, is during a war. During a war there's going to be a humanitarian crisis but it was a humanitarian crisis caused by Hamas's failure to abide by the ceasefire and its sending rockets to kill Israeli civilians.

So what my hope is that the media look more deeply at the cycle and the causes and the tactic used by Hamas and not just look at the dead bodies that are being held up.

Dershowitz: While we're waiting for questions may I add one point to what was previously said?

Jennifer Packer: Yes, please do.

Dershowitz: I think another point that has to be made is that when former President Carter appears on television he always appears alone. Although he wrote his first book, and presumably his second book saying that he wanted to provoke a debate, as you probably all know he's refused a debate. When Brandeis University invited him to debate or discuss the book with me or other knowledgeable people he's refused to do that. And he takes advantage of the fact that he's often on television with commentators who just don't know the issue as well as other people might know the issue and I would think it would be a very useful thing for Jimmy Carter to be open to debate. I offered to come down to the Carter Center at my own expense and sit down and have a conversation with him in front of an audience and he's refused to allow that. Indeed, the Carter Center has even refused to allow me to speak and present an alternative point of view to Carter's even without former President Carter on the stage. So I think a debate would be a very good thing.

Kenneth Stein: And Alan let me just add. When he gives his public presentations to universities, he does it according to his rules of engagement. His rules of engagement are that questions must be submitted on the 3 x 5 card; they must be filtered through a dean, a president or a provost and there is no follow-up. So just because a question is asked doesn't mean it's—the question is answered by Carter and therefore you really don't get into discussion about the issues and you can't hold him accountable

Dershowitz: Indeed there are several specific questions that President Carter has refused to answer even though he's been asked at virtually every university that he's been at. Namely he said after the fact that he thought it was the right thing for Yasser Arafat to turn down the two-state solution, turn down statehood, turn down the Clinton-Barack offer; and we know that President Carter was advising Yasser Arafat at many points regarding his relationship with the United States, and it would seem likely that President Carter gave Yasser Arafat that same advice before the fact as he did after the fact, namely that it would be suicidal for any Palestinian leader to accept a peace treaty with Israel based on the Camp David and Taba Accord. He's refused to answer that question.

Davis: Are there any questions? This is Lanny Davis. I'll serve as a moderator, be able to answer your question, or ask Professor Dershowitz or Professor Stein to answer.

Robert Ledeen: Yes, hello. The distortions of Jimmy Carter are well known, and the questions that many of us have is what is his motivation. I wonder if any of you can address that, and a particular question. Is his center, I think it's in Atlanta (inaudible). Is it funded by any of the countries or groups that are hating and desiring to destroy Israel?

Davis: Let me jump in as the moderator. We do not answer questions about people's motivations. We are not psychiatrists nor do we impugn people's motives. We assume that President Carter is sincere, but we just disagree with him, and we're here to talk about his omissions of fact or his statements of facts that are not correct.

Ken Stein: When I was executive director of the center we took money from very wealthy Jews in Atlanta. We took money from the Japanese. We took money from the Europeans. We took money from the Saudis. We took money from just about anyone in order to build a center. We took money from the Rockefeller Foundation, the Koret Foundation, and in the early program no one ever directed me to do something that was particularly pro-Israeli or pro-Zionist or anti-Israeli or anti-Zionist. We were told really to just go out and do some academic work to bring in people who would represent all points of view. Now that was in the '80s. Once we got to the middle of the '90s things changed at the Carter Center, and I would argue that if you ask academic interns who've been at the Carter Center now for the last four or five years, those who come from all over the world to work as interns, they will tell you that in any presentation that Carter gives about the Middle East they are not allowed to confront him on an issue if they disagree with Carter's view of how the Middle East works and operates. I've actually had Carter Center interns at my dinner table who have gone on record telling me that the Carter Center is not any more a place where you go to try and resolve differences. It's a place where you go and try and put the burden of the responsibility on Israel. Whether that comes from funding I do not know. Whether that's because Carter has turned a corner and gone in a different direction that much I can say. I know he's not the man he was when I was working with him in the early '80s.

Dershowitz: I can add one thing to that, and that is several years ago Sheikh Zayed Bin Sultan Al Nahyan gave a $3 million contribution to the Harvard Divinity School, which was sorely in need of money; and of course Harvard checked him out and discovered that he was a Holocaust denier, conspiracy theorist, and an anti-Semite who claimed that, quote, "Zionists and not Nazis killed the Jews of Europe." Harvard returned the money. President Carter received a large grant from Zayed. Not only did he accept it, but upon receiving the money he gave a speech and he said the following. "This award has special significance for me because it is named for my personal friend Sheikh Zayed Bin Sultan Al Nahyan"—a Holocaust denier and a man who offers these conspiracy theories. Again I agree with Lanny, I can't get into the heart and soul of any person, but I think the facts speak for themselves.

Ledeen: Yes. Thank you.

Davis: Do we have any other questions from reporters from news organizations, please?

Operator: Our next question comes from Nathan Gutman with *The Forward.*

Nathan Gutman: Thank you. Hi. This is Nathan Gutman from *The Forward.* I have two questions, and my first question is do you think that Carter can play any constructive role in the Middle East? In the past he tried to speak, or he said he tried to speak with the Hamas leaders in Damascus about releasing Gilad Shalit. Do you think in the future he might be seen as a possible mediator on this issue? And the second question is that in regarding President Obama and his ties with Jimmy Carter in Palestine I believe it was this week on the Daily Show actually that he believed that Obama was, promote peace in the Middle East. Do you have any indication as to whether Carter is advising Obama or whether Obama is speaking to Carter on these issues?

Dershowitz: Well I know for sure that he is not advising him. We've heard directly from President Obama that he's not accepting advice either from Jimmy Carter or from his Former Secretary of State Brzezinski regarding Israel. He said that during the campaign as clearly as possible. One has to note also that I think for the first time in American history a former president did not speak at the Democratic Convention, and that president was Jimmy Carter. Yes, I think Jimmy Carter could play a role if he could help release an Israeli prisoner. Sure by all means, the same way that Jesse Jackson has tried to do that; but he cannot play any role in negotiations generally about the peace process. He's disqualified himself from doing that by taking a strident side. The Israeli government would have no faith or trust in him, but if he can help resolve issues involving prisoners or if he can talk to Hamas, God bless him, let him do it, of course.

I was with Jimmy Carter in Israel on the day of the election that elected Hamas to office, and it was a legitimate election. I observed the election, so did Jimmy Carter observe the election. He predicted to me the day before the election that there was nothing to worry about; Hamas would be resoundedly defeated at the polls. Of course his prediction doesn't appear in his writings because he turned out to be wrong, but Hamas did win the election, and you know many people misinterpret that by saying Hamas won the election therefore they're not just a terrorist group.

The point is they won an election. Therefore every rocket sent from Hamas is an act of the government of Gaza, and an armed attack under Charter Article 51 of the United Nations; and the people of Gaza bear more responsibility obviously than they would if just some gang of hoodlums was sending rockets over the border. Not that that justifies any kind of deliberate civilian deaths, and there have been no deliberate civilian deaths caused by Israel; but when people vote for somebody as the Germans voted for Adolph Hitler in 1933 and he was the legitimate leader of Germany, the people who vote for war instead of peace bear accountability and responsibility, and tend to suffer more than when people are captive of a tyrant who simply was imposed upon them; and people forget that the people of Gaza voted overwhelmingly for Hamas, and they have paid a very heavy price for that; and one hopes that any peace process with the West Bank will create a West Bank of peace and prosperity and educational opportunity, much like West Berlin, and then the people of Palestine could see that making peace and giving up dreams of destroying Israel pay a tremendous peace dividend and remaining with Hamas does not pay that kind of dividend, and results in the kind of life that many are tragically living in the Gaza today.

Andrew Silow-Carroll: Hi It's Andrew Silow-Carroll from *New Jersey Jewish News.* I've seen Carter interviewed twice now on this book, and just in his message that Israel and Palestine will be side by side with Israel's right to exist recognized by its neighbors, Israel withdrawing to its 1967 borders, and then he'll say that's basically the policy of Kadima and the Israeli government. I'm trying to gauge what, and I understood how the first book was provocative starting with its title and much of its, some of the distortions in the content; but what's prompting your upset at this moment with this book? How is the plan that he is putting forward seem more troublesome or mischievous than kind of the inevitable two-state solution that everyone is talking about including the Obama government and the Israeli government?

Dershowitz: I find myself in a strange situation because I find myself completely agreeing with Jimmy Carter's results, the two-state solution, yes, negotiating the two-state solution, yes. I also happen to agree with him that President Obama sending George Mitchell as a negotiator is a good thing. I also think that the settlements on the West Bank have to end. So I don't find myself in disagreement very much with Jimmy Carter's end game. I find myself in considerable disagreement with how he proposes to get there; I think he's become a barrier to peace because by supporting essentially Hamas and by not exposing the Hamas tactic and by letting Hamas be victorious when it uses this tactic of provoking Israel into responding, hiding behind civilians, then the media attacking Israel and Jimmy Carter becoming part of that, I think he makes peace more difficult to achieve. So my disagreements with Carter are not about the end game. I wish it were as inevitable as some of my colleagues think it is. I don't think it's that inevitable anymore, but my real criticism of Carter is that he makes it much harder for peace to be achieved by siding with Hamas and against Israel and becoming part of that chorus of condemnation every time Israel responds in self defense, and thereby encouraging Hamas to continue to send rockets, which by the way in his first book he refused to categorize as terrorism at all. He then had to apologize for that.

Operator: Our next question comes from Mark Finkelstein with the Jewish Federation of Des Moines.

Mark Finkelstein: Yes, hi. Mark Finkelstein. Hello. Mr. Dershowitz you've mentioned in explaining about the blockade that one of the reasons was to put pressure on the Palestinian people who elected a terrorist government. Our adversaries will claim that's collective punishment and use it against us. What do you think?

Dershowitz: Well no, it's not collective punishment. In democracies people are accountable for the actions of their leaders. It was not collective punishment for the United States and Great Britain to insist on unconditional surrender of Germany. It was not collective punishment for the United States to insist on unconditional surrender of Japan. People pay consequences when they vote for warfare, and again I remind you of the quote from Fathi Hamad, for the Palestinian people death has become an industry. He claims to be talking for the Palestinian people when he says that women and children are used as shields. We have to distinguish between women and children. Many women have been used as terrorists. Many women have been used as voluntary human shields. Once you become a human shield you're a combatant whether you're a man or a woman or you're 17 years old or you're 15 years old, but not when you're five years old; and that's why Israel goes to such great efforts to try to prevent that; and what Israel is doing is not punishing. What it's doing is it's imposing a blockade to prevent rockets from coming in.

Remember too that when Germany came to power there were efforts to try to have sanctions against Nazi Germany in the 1930s. Was that collective punishment? In my book about terrorism I talk about a continuum of collectivity of punishment, and you know if you deliberately hurt somebody or kill somebody, that's collective punishment; but not if you do what happened in East Berlin when life was more difficult to the East Berliners and better for West Berlin because the world should see that being part of a free Western democracy as West Berlin was is better than being subject to the tyranny of communism. Sure. People pay consequences for sides that they're on, and particularly when they elect as they did Hamas and the way they accept Hamas there are going to be consequences. That's not collective punishment. That's the reality of life.

May I add one other point about collective punishment. Namely if you want to talk about collective punishment, the efforts by Canadian academics, by British academics, by French academics to impose boycotts against all Israeli academics, that's collective punishment, and those who complained about Israel are the ones, the first ones to engage in collective punishment. Hamas believes in destroying all the Jewish people. That's collective punishment. Hamas aims rockets at Jewish children. That's collective punishment, and it doesn't compare at all to Israel perhaps depriving some people in the Gaza of, again to quote the *New York Times,* snacks like chocolate chips and sodas. That's not collective punishment.

Davis: All right. Thank you all very much, and I appreciate your participation in this conference call.

Chapter 15
Why I Hate The Hard Left But Won't Join the Right: An Answer to Dennis Prager

During the course of the conflict in Gaza, conservative columnist Dennis Prager praised me for my stance on Israel but criticized me for remaining a liberal democrat. I responded to him as follows.

My old friend Dennis Prager can't understand why I don't leave the left to join him on the right. Let me explain. I am a civil libertarian, centrist liberal who supports most of the policies of mainstream Democrats and opposes many of the policies of the Republican Party and of conservatives. I support progressive taxation. I oppose tax breaks to the rich, even though I am relatively affluent. I support the right of working people and unions, though I oppose efforts by some unions to deny their members anonymous voting rights. I strongly support the separation of church and state. Indeed, I would build a wall of separation even higher than it is now, consistent with the principles of Jefferson and Madison. I strongly oppose efforts by many Republicans and conservatives to lower the wall, to Christianize America and to argue that atheists and agnostics are less moral than believers in traditional religion. I strongly favor stem cell research and complete equality for homosexuals. I support a woman's right to choose under most circumstances. I favor a broad reading of the constitutional rights of those accused of crime, even terrorism, and oppose efforts, whether by Republicans or Democrats to circumvent the constitution or to operate beneath the radar screen of accountability. I strongly favor our system of checks and balances and oppose the Republican concept of the "unitary executive." I favor a maximalist view of freedom of speech and oppose efforts to censor pornography, blasphemy or other "objectionable" forms of speech. I favor strict regulation of gun ownership, consistent with the Second Amendment. I favor universal health care consistent with maintaining the high quality of medicine. I support the kind of free college education afforded me at the New York City college system.

I spend much of my life fighting against the bigotry of the hard left when it comes to Israel and American foreign policy. My staunchest enemies in the world include Noam Chomsky. Norman Finkelstein, Tony Judd, Elon Pappe, Alexander Cockburn, Jimmy Carter and others on the hard left who are obsessed with Israel's imperfections, while ignoring genocides and real abuses of human rights in other parts of the world. As a centrist liberal and Democrat, I believe I have a special obligation to attack the hard left, because my attacks receive somewhat more credibility than the attacks coming from the right. (I also believe that conservative supporters of Israel have a special obligation to attack those on the hard right, such as Pat Buchanan and Robert Novak, who are virulently anti-Israel.)

Moreover, I base my defense of Israel on liberal values. I support Israel precisely because it is a secular democracy (I wish it had more of the separation between synagogue and state), because of its commitment to human rights and civil liberties, because of its adherence to the concept of holiness of arms (in the secular sense), because it fights defensive rather than aggressive wars. I support Israel because of its generally progressive views on women, gays, the environment and civil liberties. I am an admirer of Israeli's Supreme Court.

Nor am I alone in being a centrist liberal democrat who supports Israel. I work with Irwin Cotler, a member of the Canadian Liberal Party and former Minister of Justice, with Elie Wiesel, with

Anthony Julius of London, with Sam Pisar in Paris, with Amos Oz and Aaron Barak in Israel and with many others in academia and politics. My views are close to those of Ted Kennedy, Bill Clinton, Hillary Clinton, Joe Biden, Al Gore, Barney Frank—and I hope Barack Obama.

It is extraordinarily important for Israel to be supported by the left and the right. Support for Israel should never become a conservative cause alone, a mission of only the religious right and a plank of only the Republican Party. It must remain a bipartisan issue. On college campuses as well, there must be liberal supporters of Israel to counteract the many hard left Israel bashers.

It is the hard left that has left the left over Israel. My goal is to increase support for Israel within the mainstream of Democrats and liberals. I will not be kicked out of the left by its anti-Israel extremist fringe. I will instead continue to support Israel to attack those on the hard left who demonize Israel, and to support centrist liberal principles that are good for America, for Jews and for the entire world.

Chapter 16
Frontpage Interview

During and after the fighting in Gaza, Frontpage Magazine *asked me to respond to questions about the ongoing situation. Here is the exchange:*

Frontpage Interview's guest today is Alan M. Dershowitz, the Felix Frankfurter Professor of Law at Harvard Law School. His latest book is *The Case Against Israel's Enemies: Exposing Jimmy Carter and Others Who Stand in the Way of Peace.*

FP: What were the key issues on your mind during the Gaza war?

Dershowitz: Hamas figured out how to win a media victory by sacrificing its own civilians. It was committing a double war crime by targeting Israeli civilians from behind Palestinian human shields. This despicable and unlawful tactic could never have succeeded without the complicity of the United Nations, many in the European community, the hard left and much of the media.

FP: What was Hamas's goal in the war?

Dershowitz: The goal of Hamas was to produce as many dead Palestinian women and children as possible and to have the media show these victims uncritically and without asking who was to blame. So there were many villains to this piece and yet Israel, which was acting entirely lawfully and in self-defense, bore the brunt of international criticism. This only encouraged Hamas, Hezbollah and Israel's other enemies to repeat this tactic over and over again, because for the terrorists, it's a win-win situation and for democracies, it's a lose-lose situation.

FP: No other nation in history has dealt as humanely, and with such compassion, in its fight against terrorism as Israel. And yet, as you point out, it bears the brunt of international criticism. Why? What explains this phenomenon?

Dershowitz: There are several explanations. First is that the Hamas tactic of inducing Israel to kill Palestinian civilians by using them as human shields works at least on some people. But there are deeper factors at work. Many people, especially in Europe, look for excuses to hate Israel. They love to hate the Jewish state. Part of the reason is the close relationship between Israel and the United States. Part of the reason is that Israel is the Jew among nations and anti-Semites respond to the Jewish nation in the same way that they respond to the Jewish people. Finally, many young people are subjected to constant propaganda by their teachers, many of whom come from the hard left.

FP: Iran and Hezbollah decided to sit this war out. How come in your view?

Dershowitz: Because they can win without lifting a finger. They supply the rockets to Hamas. They complain loudly. They rattle a few swords and they sit back and laugh at how easily the media is manipulated in the service of terrorism.

FP: The media is easily manipulated in the service of terrorism because it is controlled by liberal elites—who are biased against the U.S. and Israel. Right?

Dershowitz: I don't agree with that statement. I think that even neutral journalists are impacted by the Hamas strategy. It is extraordinarily effective because it works on emotion and not reason.

FP: Is there actually any real hope for a two-state solution?

Dershowitz: There was great hope for a two-state solution when Clinton and Barack offered it to the Palestinians in 2000. But as Prince Bandar of Saudi Arabia correctly put it, Arafat committed a crime against the Palestinian people by turning down the offer. Arafat wanted to see the end of the Jewish state more than he wanted to see the establishment of a Palestinian state. When the Palestinian leadership and a substantial majority of the Palestinian people want their own state more than they want the end of the Jewish state, there will be a two-state solution. There is no real alternative to the two-state solution, except continuing warfare.

FP: What do you think of the demographic trends that appear to threaten the future of Israel?

Dershowitz: The demographic trends are an important reason why Israel should actively seek a two-state solution. If a successful Palestinian state will emerge—a state with freedom, economic potential and peacefulness—many of the Arab citizens of Israel might eventually choose to move there. That must be their choice. Right now almost no Israeli Arabs want to move to Palestine because life in Israel is so much better for them than it is in any Arab state.

FP: When you refer to a "successful Palestinian state" that might emerge that will have "freedom, economic potential and peacefulness," how optimistic are you that this is possible? It's a wonderful scenario of course, but do you really believe that Palestinians, with their death-cult culture and their Islamist supporters who lust for Jewish blood, will one day somehow be able to accept Jews as neighbours and choose a democratic and peaceful way of life?

Dershowitz: Yes. The culture of life is more powerful than the culture of death.

FP: Your thoughts on the world's reaction to Israel's attempt to defend itself in the Gaza war?

Dershowitz: The reaction of much of the world was not only morally despicable but played right into the hands of terrorists. It encouraged terrorists to persist in their double war crime tactic and to use civilians as pawns.

FP: Tell us a bit about some of the criticisms of you and what you think of them.

Dershowitz: I'm generally proud of the criticism directed at me because it tends to come from some of the worst people in the world: the neo-Nazi hard right and the neo-Stalinist hard left. It tends to be *ad hominem,* thoughtless, non-substantive and often overtly bigoted. What does concern me is when otherwise thoughtful people fall for the Hamas tactic and allow their emotional reaction to terrible images to skew their rational views. I was particularly disappointed in Bill Moyers' equation of Israeli self-defense to Hamas terrorism. He said it was "exactly the same." Shame on him.

FP: Your thoughts on Norman Finkelstein and Noam Chomsky? What impulses, in your view, motivate Jewish individuals to reach out in solidarity to those forces under whose power they would be annihilated?

Dershowitz: Norman Finkelstein is a sick and deeply disturbed, self-hating Jew, who in his autobiography implied that his own mother was a kappo. He constantly compares Israel to the Nazis (though he seems to admire the Nazis and to despise Israel). [In an article published in the *Iranian Times,* he calls Israel satanic and demonic and characterizes Israeli self-defense actions as a Holocaust—this from a man who accepted Ahmadinejad's invitation to speak at the notorious Holocaust denial "conference" in Tehran several years ago.] He constantly invokes anti-Semitic stereotypes of the kind that were found in *Der Stürmer.* He is beneath contempt and deserves no further comment. He should be relegated to the dustbin of history and ignored. Chomsky, on the other hand, is a serious linguist, but a total ignoramus and bigot when it comes to Israel. He must be taken seriously and answered in the marketplace of ideas. That's why I always accept invitations to debate Chomsky.

FP: Jimmy Carter was at it again during the war. I'm sure you saw his *Washington Post* piece: "An Unecessary War." Carter referred to Hamas as if it was some kind of social welfare agency that was bullied into taking up arms. It's as if Article XI in their Charter doesn't exist, and as if Hamas has some reason for its existence other than the annihilation of Israel. Carter referred to "a defensive tunnel" being dug by Hamas. And this is not, apparently, some kind of morbid and twisted sense of humor on Carter's part. What gives here? What's the psychology of a man like this?

Dershowitz: Jimmy Carter has been completely bought and paid for by extremist Islamic money. He has accepted funding from Holocaust deniers, who he had characterized as friends. He seems to love tyrants such as Arafat, Assad, and the leaders of Hamas and Hezbollah, but he seems to despise virtually all Israeli leaders. He also seems afflicted by a perverse form of deep-seated theological anti-Judaism. I have written extensively about him in my book "The Case Against Israel's Enemies: Exposing Jimmy Carter and Others Who Stand In The Way of Peace."

FP: Your advice for Israel and the Obama administration in terms of how to deal with the Mideast issue—in the context of Hamas, Fatah, Hezbollah and Iran?

Dershowitz: I hope that Barack Obama follows through with what he said as a presidential candidate. He should try to achieve peace through negotiations. He should be tough on Israel when it comes to non-security issues, such as civilian settlements deep in the West Bank. But he should support Israel in its legitimate efforts to defend itself from terrorism and from the existential threat posed by Iran's nuclear weapons program.

FP: Will the Obama administration be a true friend of Israel?

Dershowitz: There is every reason to hope and expect that he will be, based on what he said during the campaign and who he has appointed to serve in his administration.

FP: But what of his appointment of George Mitchell and seeming reaching out to Fatah and Abbas?

Dershowitz: I support that.

FP: Do you give the Bush administration credit for its support of Israel?

Dershowitz: I give the Bush administration great credit for its support of Israel, but it took actions which hurt Israel and failed to take some actions that would have helped Israel. The war in Iraq, which then Prime Minister Ariel Sharon opposed, has been a disaster for Israel, since it has diverted attention away from Israel's existential enemy, Iran. I wish that Bush had picked up where Clinton had left off and tried to initiate active peace efforts earlier on in his first term. I do think that George Bush's heart is in the right place when it comes to Israel.

FP: Well, for the record, in Iraq the Bush administration overthrew a fascist dictator and ended up defeating Al Qaeda there. The surge succeeded, sectarian violence is now down, and Iraq is moving in a positive direction. In this success, which one will never read about in the mainstream media, America has dealt a deadly blow to our enemy in the terror war.

But this debate belongs in another forum—and the point cannot be denied that any diversion of attention away from dealing with Iran is a bad thing.

It is questionable how Bush can be criticized for not picking up where Clinton had left off in terms of the peace process. The Bush administration didn't stop the "peace" process; Arafat did. As your own work has demonstrated, Mr. Dershowitz, Arafat rejected Barack's over-generous offer and called for a new Intifada. What many had suspected became undeniably clear: from the very beginning of Oslo, Arafat had never been serious about real peace. All throughout the peace process, he continued to support terror against Israel and to oversee the ideological indoctrination of his own people—which propagated the illegitimacy of Israel and the necessity of its annihilation. The Palestinians clearly remained more interested in destroying the Jewish state than in creating their own.

The Bush administration understood that the Palestinians had to shed themselves of their terrorist infrastructure and ideology before any real peace process could be renewed. It would have been simply absurd and destructive for Bush to have continued Arafat's sick charade. No?

Dershowitz: Yes, but as soon as Arafat met his untimely death—untimely in the sense that if he had died five years *earlier* we might have had a two-state solution—the Bush Administration should have moved aggressively to make peace with Abbas.

FP: Final thoughts?

Dershowitz: I love tough questions. And you asked some mighty tough ones.

FP: Alan Dershowitz, thank you for joining *Frontpage Interview*.

Dershowitz: Thank you.

Chapter 17
The Moral Blindness of Some "Religious Leaders"

In my interview with Frontpage, *I briefly referred to Bill Moyers. In the following article posted on* The Jerusalem Post, *I provided a detailed criticism of his views and those of other so-called "religious leaders" when it comes to Israel.*

Bill Moyers holds himself out to be a moral arbiter, based in large part on his commitment to Christian principles. Cardinal Renato Martino is an official of the Catholic church and President of the Council for Justice and Peace. Former President Jimmy Carter preaches peace, based on the teachings of Jesus. Yet when it comes to the conflict between Israel and Hamas, all three are morally blind.

In a widely watched television assessment of the recent conflict in Gaza, here is what Moyers said: "By killing indiscriminately the elderly, kids, entire families, by destroying schools and hospitals, Israel *did exactly* what terrorists do..." (emphasis added) Of course he also included the obligatory hedge that: "Every nation has the right to defend its people."

Cardinal Martino went even further, making an obscene and historically ignorant, comparison between Israel's self-defense actions against rockets fired by Hamas at Israeli children, and the Nazi genocide against the Jews during the Holocaust. He said that the conditions in Gaza "resembles a big concentration camp." Concentration camps, of course, were places where Jews were held until they could be processed through the machinery of death, as part of a massive genocidal program that willfully murdered 6 million Jews. Any comparison between Israel's action in Gaza and those of Nazis during the Holocaust is not only obscene, it is blatantly anti-Semitic, which is supposed to be a sin under Vatican law. (It is apparently not, however, a sin for a Catholic bishop to deny that the Holocaust occurred at all, since Bishop Richard Williamson of Great Britain was welcomed back into the Catholic church after claiming that there were no gas chambers and that the Jews are lying when they say that 6 million of them were killed, when, according to that bigoted bishop, a mere 300,000 Jews died during the entire Holocaust. The batty bishop—who, like the Taliban, opposes higher education for women—also believes that no airplanes were involved in the 9/11 attack and that the buildings were blown up by explosives and rockets, presumably set and fired by the United States and Israel. To its belated credit, the Vatican—after being widely criticized by many good Catholics—demanded that Williamson renounce his Holocaust denial.)

An essential aspect of Christian teaching, and especially of Catholic teaching, is the important principle that distinguishes between intentionally killing an innocent person, and unintentionally killing an innocent person in the process of legitimately trying to prevent harm to one's self or others. This concept, known as the principle of double effect, is central to Catholic theology. It traces its roots to Thomas Aquinas and has had enormous influence on moral thinking not only within the Catholic Church, but throughout Christianity and indeed in the secular world as well. Understanding and complying with this principle may literally mean the difference between eternal damnation and eternal salvation. That's how important it is.

Except, apparently, when it comes to the Jewish state of Israel. Then suddenly moral blindness makes it impossible for church authorities to see, understand or apply this principle. Cardinal Martino is not the first church leader to try to create moral equivalence between the actions of

Hamas in willfully and proudly trying to kill as many Jewish children, women and other civilians as possible, and the actions of the Israeli Defense Forces in trying to stop them from killing Jewish children, while inadvertently killing some Palestinian civilians who are used as human shields by Hamas. The Pope himself has been guilty of invoking such moral equivalence between these very different actions. Indeed it is fair to say that the Vatican's entire approach to the Israel-Hamas conflict has been to suggest a false moral equivalence.

Church leaders know better. They understand precisely what they are doing. They are making utilitarian, pragmatic and very anti-Catholic cynical judgments calculated to bolster the influence of the Church in the Middle East. It might be understandable for secular nations to act in so amoral if not immoral, a manner, but it is entirely unacceptable for the Catholic church, which eschews utilitarianism and preaches moral consistency and moral absolutism, to act in so cynical a way.

This is especially troubling, because the church tends to forget its own teachings primarily when it deals with the Jewish people and the Jewish state. Its long history of discrimination and bigotry against Jews—slaughtering entire Jewish communities on the way to the Crusades, murdering entire Jewish communities during the inquisitions, fomenting pogroms, signing a pact with Hitler during the Holocaust, harboring Nazi war criminals after the war, being among the last to recognize Israel—should make it even more concerned about applying a double standard of morality to the Jewish state. But that's exactly what it does. And then it complains when critics point to this obvious double standard.[12]

This abusive Christian teaching is not limited to the Catholic church. Bill Moyers and Jimmy Carter both hold themselves out as exemplary Protestants, whose morality derives from the teachings of Jesus. Yet they too create false moral equivalence between willful murder, and self-defense that sometimes results in accidental killings because Hamas deliberately uses human shields in order to make it impossible for Israel to defend its own civilians without occasionally killing Palestinian civilians. How else could one read Moyers statement that what Israel did "was exactly what terrorists do." Exactly? Well not exactly! Not even close. As different as anything could be based on principles that Moyers' espouses in other contexts. Listen to a leading military expert—retired British Colonel Richard Kemp—who concluded that there has been "no time in the history of warfare when an Army has made more efforts to reduce civilian casualties...than the Israel Defense Forces in Gaza." Is that "exactly what terrorists do," Mr. Moyers?

Jimmy Carter is even worse. He doesn't even see moral *equivalence.* He blames everything on Israel. Jimmy Carter should look in the mirror more often and he will see that he himself bears much of the blame for the death and destruction that he deplores. In his book, *Palestine: Peace Not Apartheid,* he says it would have been "suicidal" for Yasser Arafat to accept the generous offer made by Bill Clinton and Ehud Barak at Camp David and Taba. Remember that that offer included independent statehood for the Palestinian people on all of the Gaza and 97% or 98% of the West Bank, an end to Jewish settlements, no checkpoints, a Palestinian capital in East Jerusalem and a $35 billion refugee reparation package. Think for a moment of what Carter is saying when he warns that any Palestinian leader who might accept such an offer would be assassinated. What is he saying about the Palestinian people? That they will never accept peace without violence? That they will always kill their leaders who make peace with Israel, as the Muslim brotherhood murdered Anwar Sadat of Egypt, and as Muslim extremists killed the first King Abdullah of Jordan. Whether he advised Yasser Arafat before the fact to reject the Camp David offer, which the evidence strongly suggests,[13] or whether he is merely making that suggestion to future Palestinian leaders, he has clearly become a barrier to peace. If he in fact told Arafat to reject the offer, then he is an important contributing cause to the current crisis.

The sad reality is that religious doctrines are as easily manipulated by cynical churchmen as anything Jeremy Bentham ever proposed in the name of utilitarianism.

Bill Moyers ended a letter to the *New York Times* in which he defended his moral equivalency statement by saying that to be indifferent to suffering is "to be as blind as Sampson in Gaza." No, Mr. Moyers, to be indifferent to the crucial difference between what terrorists do, namely try to kill as many civilians as possible from behind human shields, and what democracies such as Israel and the United States do, namely try to stop terrorists from killing with the minimum possible injury to civilians, is truly to be "eyeless in Gaza."

---

[12] Alan Dershowitz, *The Case Against Israel's Enemies: Exposing Jimmy Carter and Others Whoe Stand in the Way of Peace,* Hoboken: John Wiley & Sons, 2008, 180-82.

[13] On March 20 and 21, 2007, the New York Times reported on disturbing allegations made to a "left-leaning" newspaper by some Israeli soldiers regarding the conduct of other Israeli soldiers during the Gaza War. These allegations reported by an institute headed by someone "known to be on the left of Israel's political spectrum" included the general claim that the IDF had failed to comply with its usual ethical duty to "avoid civilian casualties" even when "that involves taking some risk." A company commander disputed this claim, noting that "we put soldiers at risk to prevent harming their civilians." The military advocate general immediately began an investigation. Other civilian agencies will investigate as well.

Chapter 18
For the International Criminal Court To Work, The Worst Must Come First

Following the cease fire, the Palestinian Authority, Jordan, Bolivia and others called for the International Criminal Court in The Hague to open an investigation of Israeli war crimes. I wrote the following article in response.

There are efforts now underway to try to bring Israel before the International Criminal Court (ICC) in the Hague on charges of alleged war crimes. Neither Israel nor the United States has signed on to this court, primarily out of fear that its power would be used against democracies that try their best to avoid war crimes, rather than against dictatorships and terrorist nations that routinely engage in them. This has certainly been the experience with many United Nations organizations, even including the International Court of Justice, which is largely a sham when it comes to Israel and other democracies under attack.

There has been high hope among some human rights experts that the ICC would be different for two reasons: First and foremost it is not a United Nations court. It was established by the Rome Statute, a treaty adopted in 1998 after years of negotiations, and is largely independent of the United Nations, though not completely so. Cases can be referred to it by the UN Security Council under Article 13(b) of the treaty. The second reason the ICC has encouraged optimism is that the person appointed as the court's Chief Prosecutor, Luis Moreno-Ocompo, has a sterling reputation for objective law enforcement and basic fairness.

The ICC has rightly opened up investigations of genocide in Darfur, Sudan. It is also looking into some other nations. It has not opened investigations with regard to Russia's alleged war crimes in Chechnya and Georgia, where thousands of innocent civilians were killed. Nor has it opened investigations with regard to Pakistan, Afghanistan, Sri Lanka, Zimbabwe, and other places where civilians are routinely targeted as part of military and terrorist campaigns. Nor—to its credit—has it opened an investigation of Great Britain and the United States, whose armed forces have inadvertently caused the deaths of thousands of civilians in Iraq and Afghanistan.

Were it now to open an investigation of Israel, the ICC would be violating the cardinal principle that must govern all international prosecutions: namely, that the worst must be prosecuted first. It would also be violating its own rules which mandate that the International Criminal Court will not become a substitute for domestic courts. If there are processes within the State of Israel to consider allegations against the Israel Defense Forces (IDF), then those processes must be allowed to move forward unless Israel is "unwilling or unable genuinely to carry out the investigation or prosecution," according to the Rome Statute. There is no country in the world—literally none—that has a judicial system that is more open to charges against its own government. Not the United States, not Great Britain, and certainly not Russia, Zimbabwe or Pakistan! Moreover, Israel has a completely open and very critical free press, which is constantly exposing Israeli imperfections and editorializing against them. Third, the IDF has legal teams that must approve of every military action taken by the armed forces. There are obviously close questions, about which reasonable experts can disagree, but there is no country in the world that goes to greater lengths in its efforts to conform its military actions to international law. Listen to retired British Colonel Richard Kemp—a military expert who, based on his experience, concluded that there has been "no time in the history of warfare when an Army has made more efforts to reduce civilian casualties...than [the Israel Defense Forces in Gaza]."

Despite deliberate efforts by Hamas to maximize Palestinian civilian casualties by firing rockets from behind human shields, Israel has succeeded in its efforts to minimize civilian casualties. Hamas has a policy of exaggerating civilian casualties, both by inflating the total number of people killed and by reducing the number of its combatants included in that total. This week, the UN withdrew claims made during the war that Israel had shelled a school run in Gaza by the UN Relief and Works Agency.

The same Rome Statute that established the ICC also proscribes many of Hamas's actions during the war, such as attacking Israeli civilians and using Palestinian civilians as human shields. Any fair investigation by the ICC would have to conclude that Israel's efforts to prevent civilian casualties, while seeking to protect its civilians from Hamas war crimes, rank it at the very top of nations in compliance with the rule of law. It would also conclude that efforts to brand Israel's actions as war crimes are crassly political, based on ideology and not law. If anything, Hamas belongs in the dock, not Israel.

The prosecutor of the ICC must resist pressures—from the United Nations, from radical ideologues and from other biased sources—to apply a double standard to Israel by singling the Jewish state out from among law-abiding democracies for a war crimes investigation. No international court can retain its credibility if it inverts the principle of "the worst first" and instead goes after one of the best as one its first.

Chapter 19
Judge a Nation by How it Responds to its Mistakes

One of the criteria for the International Criminal Court to investigate crimes is whether the nation charged is "unwilling or unable genuinely to carry out the investigation or prosecution."

I wrote the following article to show that Israel is fully capable of investigating and prosecuting crimes when they occur.

Israel is unique among nations in the way it investigates its own mistakes and allegations of criminal conduct among its soldiers and leaders. When then General Ariel Sharon was accused of inaction in failing to stop Lebanese Christian Falangists in Lebanon from slaughtering Palestinians in Sabra and Shatila, Israel immediately set up an investigatory commission. Despite Sharon's enormous popularity, the commission found him at fault for failing to stop the crimes committed by the Falangists. (Lebanon, on the other hand, did little to investigate the actual murderers or the murder that provoked the revenge killings.) Other commissions, usually headed by retired Supreme Court justices, have investigated other Israeli mistakes and crimes.

Moreover, the Israeli Supreme Court is open to complaints by all alleged victims of Israeli crimes or unlawful policies, and they frequently rule in favor of Palestinian litigants and against the Israeli government. It is far more open than American or European courts, which have limitations such as "standing" requirements, "political question" doctrines and other barriers to judicial review.

Israel routinely investigates and frequently prosecutes soldiers for violating the high standards of warfare imposed by the IDF's Code of Ethics. For example, Israel is investigating the firing of two tank shells on January 16 at the home of a Gaza doctor that killed several children. Israel-bashers immediately claimed these deaths were deliberate, willful and without any military basis. But here is how the *New York Times* reported on it:

> Also Wednesday, the Israeli military acknowledged that its soldiers fired two tank shells on Jan. 16 at the house of Izzeldin Abuelaish, a well-known Gaza doctor, killing three of his daughters and a niece.
>
> The military said it concluded from an investigation that an infantry force had come under heavy sniper and mortar fire from a house adjacent to the doctor's, and identified "suspicious figures" in the upper level of the doctor's house who were "thought to be spotters who directed the Hamas sniper and mortar fire."
>
> The doctor denied that any militants were operating from the house. The commander of the force gave the order to open fire, and Dr. Abuelaish's family members were killed as a result. The military said that in the days leading up to the episode, officers had contacted the doctor and urged him to evacuate his home because of intense fighting in the area.
>
> The military said that it was "saddened by the harm caused" to the doctor's family, but that under the circumstances, it considered the decision to fire toward the building "reasonable."
>
> The doctor has long worked in Israeli hospitals and is known as a strong advocate of

Israeli-Palestinian reconciliation, and the deaths of his relatives became a high-profile example of civilian casualties that moved many in Israel and abroad.

In a message broadcast on Israel's Channel 2 television news on Wednesday, Dr. Abuelaish, speaking in Hebrew, thanked the Israelis for carrying out an honest investigation. "We all make mistakes," he said, adding that he hoped that such a mistake would never be repeated.

Military mistakes—which always occur in the fog of war—are inevitable. Indeed more Israeli soldiers were killed in Gaza by accidental friendly fire than by deliberate enemy power. There is an enormous difference, both legally and morally, between accidental or "collateral" deaths of the kind that resulted from Israel's lawful self-defense efforts to destroy rockets and terrorists protected by human shields, and Hamas's unlawful and aggressive efforts to kill as many Israeli children as possible.

The Israeli legal system understands this difference and acts on it. It can be trusted to do more objective justice than the often biased international tribunals.

In an article in the *New York Times* on February 11, 2009, about the possibility of the International Criminal Court opening an investigation of Israel, *Human Rights Watch* said that Israel had a "poor record of investigating and prosecuting serious violations by its forces." This is totally false, as is typical of *Human Rights Watch* when it comes to Israel. I challenge HRW to name another country that has a better record of investigation and prosecution. I challenge HRW to document the claim that Israel has a poor record in comparison with other countries. If Israel's record were to be regarded as "poor," then the words of the Rome Treaty, "unwilling or unable genuinely to carry out the investigation or prosecution," would apply to every single country in the world, and would render this protection of national sovereignty utterly meaningless.

Chapter 20
What should Israel have done?

Another criteria for deciding whether a nation should be accused of crimes is whether it had other alternative ways of defending its citizens from attack. To show Israel acted reasonably, I wrote this article.

None of Israel's many critics and demonizers have as yet provided a reasonable answer to the hardest question relating to Gaza: What *should* Israel have done? That is a variation of the question that I put to many of my debate opponents during the Gaza War: What would *you* have done? Another way of putting the question is: What would the United States, Great Britain, France [fill in whatever nation you want] have done if lethal anti-personnel rockets loaded with shrapnel, were being fired randomly at civilian areas and 20% of its population were within range of those rockets?

It's easy to criticize a democratic nation for its imperfect response to a difficult situation imposed on it by terrorists who care less about life than about martyrdom. Indeed, every solution tried by Israel has been criticized.

First, Israel simply ended the occupation of the Gaza, removed the settlements, left behind greenhouses and other facilities that could have been used by the residents of Gaza to create a flourishing economy. Instead, Hamas engaged in a coup, threw out the Palestinian Authority, and brought in thousands of rockets which they randomly fired at Israeli civilian targets. They pledged to continue until "the occupation" — by which they meant any Jewish presence in Tel Aviv, Ramat Gan, Jerusalem or Haifa — ended. After the rockets began to kill, maim, and traumatize Israeli civilians, the IDF responded by targeting the terrorists who were firing the rockets and by trying to limit the ability of Hamas to import rockets from Iran. They also imposed limitations on the import of such luxury items as snacks, chocolate, soda and other non-essential and non-humanitarian goods, while allowing humanitarian essentials to pass through checkpoints.[14] Hamas responded by aiming rockets at the checkpoints themselves, thereby causing them to close for periods of time.

At the same time, Israel sought help from the international community in stopping the rockets from being fired at Israeli civilians. They received absolutely no help from the United Nations or any other international bodies. There were no protests in the streets of London, Paris or Rome about Hamas's war crimes and the impact they were having on vulnerable children.

Then Israel and Hamas agreed to a six month cease fire in the Gaza, with Israel retaining the right to retaliate against rockets fired at its civilians.

When the cease fire expired, Hamas refused to renew it and began firing large numbers of rockets, several of which barely missed Israeli schools, hospitals and civilian apartment complexes.

The Israeli government then offered a carrot and a stick: it opened up checkpoints allowing more aid to flow into Gaza; and it warned that if the rockets continued, the IDF would engage in a military operation designed to stop the rockets.

When the rockets continued, and indeed increased in frequency, Israel kept its word and began what was planned as a three-stage operation. The first stage, an air attack, lasted several days, but failed to stop the rockets. The air attack was followed by a ground invasion which also failed to stop the rockets, though it reduced their frequency. The planned third stage, a full scale invasion of urban areas from which rockets were being fired and in which Hamas leaders were hiding, was never carried out, despite the fact that rockets continued to be fired. Israel refrained from taking military action to end the rocket firings—action it was lawfully entitled to take—because it knew that Palestinian civilian casualties would be extensive.

Every one of these actions has been criticized by Israel's enemies. None of these destructive critics has offered constructive criticism—namely a reasonable alternative course of action. Surely no democracy must simply allow an enemy, whose charter calls for its destruction, to fire rockets at its children without any military response. Surely any democracy would do whatever it took to stop the rockets from endangering its children, as President Obama said at Sderot. In the absence of constructive suggestions for alternative ways that Israel could have confronted these acts of armed aggression against its civilians, it is difficult to credit much of the criticism directed at Israel's actions. And in the absence of viable, effective and better alternatives, it would be improper in the extreme to accuse Israel of engaging in war crimes when it employed the only reasonable option available to protect its civilians from war crimes.

---

[14] "Gazans argue it is out of necessity. Israel imposed an economic blockade with Hamas's takeover, limiting the flow of goods — particularly snacks like chocolate and chips and sodas — and tripling prices." [Sabrina Tavernise, "As Israeli Bombing Stops, Gazans Get Busy Rebuilding Damaged Tunnels," New York Times, Jan. 24, 2009, <http://www.nytimes.com/2009/01/24/world/middleeast/24gaza.html>.] The United Nations itself suspended aid to Gaza when Hamas was caught stealing it.

Chapter 21
How To Assure Repetition of Hamas Rocket Attacks

After the war, attention turned to avoiding a recurrence. I wrote the following article.

There is one sure-fire way of guaranteeing that Hamas will continue to employ terrorism against Israel and that other terrorist groups will increase the use of terrorism against civilians around the world. That sure-fire way is to reward the terrorists who employ this tactic and to punish their intended victims who try to fight back. This is one of the most important lessons to be learned from the recent events in Gaza, but it is not a new lesson. In 2002, I wrote a book entitled *Why Terrorism Works*. The point I made in that book is even more relevant today than it was then:

> The real root cause of terrorism is that it is successful—terrorists have consistently benefited from their terrorist acts. Terrorism will persist as long as it continues to work for those who use it, as long as the international community rewards it, as it has been doing for the past thirty-five years.

Hamas has been greatly rewarded by the international community, by human rights groups, by the media, by many academics and by millions of decent people for its indecent double war crime tactic of firing rockets at Israeli civilians from behind Palestinian human shields. And Israel has been significantly punished for trying to protect its citizens from these rockets. Although Hamas suffered a significant military defeat at the hands of the IDF, it has gained a public relations bonanza. Its status in Europe has been enhanced, as it has at the United Nations and throughout the Arab street. It lost the battle on the ground in Gaza, but may have won the war in the hearts and minds of many decent, and many more indecent, people throughout the world. And it won this war with very little cost. Whether the death toll was 500-600, as *Corriere della Sera* suggested, or 1300 as Hamas has reported, dead civilians serve the interest of Hamas, which considers them martyrs. They do not belong on the cost side of the ledger, according to the bizarre death culture that Hamas perpetuates, but rather of the benefit side of the ledger.

So here, in simple terms, is the twelve step program that Hamas and the international community should follow if it truly wants to see terrorism become the primary tactic used against democracies by those with perceived grievances.

Step 1: Use terrorism—rockets aimed at civilians, suicide bombings in pizza parlors and discothèques, bombs planted in school buses, shootings in classrooms, etc—as widely as possible against your enemies, to the point where they have no option but to respond militarily.

Step 2: Make sure that the terrorists and their weapons—rockets, explosives, etc.—are hidden among civilians in densely populated areas.

Step 3: When the inevitable attacks occur, employ human shields, the younger the better. Recruit them voluntarily, if possible, but commendeer them if necessary, even if they're babies or toddlers.

Step 4: Be certain that your terrorist fighters are wearing civilian clothing. Recruit as many women and teenage youngsters as possible to become terrorists.

Step 5: Be ready with video cameras and sympathetic journalists to videotape every single death and transmit the images as widely as possible to media outlets around the world.

Step 6: Recycle images of dead civilians, especially children, and move them from media to media, thus multiplying the number of apparently dead civilians.

Step 7: Be certain that sympathetic doctors and United Nations personnel overstate the number of civilians killed, counting every person under the age of 18 and every woman as a civilian, even if they are terrorists.

Step 8: Circulate totally false reports about civilian casualties and their location by, for example, claiming that numerous civilians were killed at a United Nations school when you know none of the dead were actually inside the school. You can be confident that the media will put your exaggerated reports on Page 1 and when the truth eventually comes out, after careful investigation days or weeks later, it will be buried in the back pages.

Step 9: Accuse the democracy of war crimes and bring cases against its leaders and soldiers in courts sympathetic to Hamas around the world. Bringing the lawsuits will create a presumption of guilt, even if the charges are dismissed months or years later.

Step 10: Schedule various United Nations "debates" at which tyrannical dictatorships from around the world line up at the podium to condemn Israel for crimes routinely committed by these dictatorships but not by Israel.

Step 11: Trot out the usual stable of reliable anti-Israel academics to flood newspapers and television shows with some of the worst drivel about international law, human rights and the laws of war—drivel that would earn students failing grades in any objective law school course on these subjects.

Step 12: Make sure that Hamas understands that if it repeats its double war crime strategy, it will once again be rewarded, and if Israel fights back, it will once again be punished.

These twelve steps are for use by terrorist groups, nations, and organizations, such as the United Nations, that seem determined to encourage terrorism.

Now here are 6 steps for those democracies that would actually like to put an end to terrorist attacks against its civilians.

Step 1: Never, under any circumstances, reward an act of terrorism or a group that employs terrorism to achieve its goals.

Step 2: Always punish terrorists and terrorists groups that employ terrorism against civilians.

Step 3: Never punish democracies that seek to prevent acts of terrorism against their civilians, especially when the terrorists hide among their own civilians in order to provoke democracies into killing civilians.

Step 4: Never allow human rights, international organizations or war crime tribunals to be hijacked by the supporters or terrorism and the enemies of democracy to punish only those who seek to protect their civilians against terrorism. This is especially true when the democracies have been patient in responding and have no reasonable alternative course other than military self-defense.

Step 5: Never manipulate the emotions of decent people by showing only the human shields who have been killed by military self-defense actions of the democracies, without explaining that it was the terrorists who caused these deaths.

Step 6: Make certain that the cause espoused by the terrorists is set back by every act of terrorism.

As I wrote in 2002:

> Not only must terrorism never be rewarded, the cause of those who employ it must be made—and must be seen to be made—worse off as a result of the terrorism than it would have been without it. The manner by which calculating terrorists define and calibrate the cost and benefits may be different from the way common criminals decide whether to rob, cheat, or bully, but society's response must be based on similar considerations. Those who employ terrorism have their own criteria for evaluating success and failure, and in implementing the immutable principle that those who employ terrorism must be worse off for having resorted to this tactic, we must make them worse off by their own criteria.

The international community, by and large, has been doing the opposite. The message it has been sending has been: keep it up. It will only help your terrorist cause and hurt your democratic enemy. No wonder Hamas, and other terrorists groups, regard their war crimes tactic as a win-win for terrorism and a lose-lose for democracy.

Chapter 22
Response to Al Aswany: New York Times

On February 8, 2005 Alla Al Aswany published at Op-Ed in the New York Times *entitled "Why the Muslim World Can't Hear Obama." In it, he argued that for the Arab street, particularly in Cairo, to be able to hear Obama, our President must "recognize what we see as a simple, essential truth: the right of people in an occupied territory to resist military occupation." In other words, Al Aswany was arguing that Hamas has the right to fire rockets at Israeli children, so long as Israel occupies any Palestinian land. Because Hamas believes that all of Israel is occupied Palestinian land, Al Aswany's position is that Hamas has the right to target Israeli children as long as Israel continues to exist. He demands that the United States "recognize" this "simple, essential truth."*

He also wrote that the Israeli self-defense actions against Hamas terrorists constituted a "massacre:" "I don't know what you call it in other languages, but in Egypt we call this a massacre."

I immediately wrote a letter in response to this effort to justify terrorism and to insist that President Obama must recognize terrorism as legitimate. The New York Times *published my letter on February 12, 2009.*

Letter to New York Times

Alla Al Aswany says that the only way the Arab street, particularly in Cairo, will hear Barak Obama is if our new president recognizes "the right of people in an occupied territory to resist military occupation." He is referring, of course, to Gaza. But it was precisely when Israel ended its occupation of Gaza that Hamas increased its rocket attacks against Israeli civilians. Alla Al Aswany conveniently forgets that the original occupier of Gaza was Egypt, between 1949 and 1967. I doubt that Mr. Al Aswany or the Cairo street would have tolerated rocket attacks from occupied Gaza against Egyptian civilian targets. If the price of the Arab street hearing President Obama is to accept terrorism as a "right" of formerly occupied people, then it is too high a price for America to pay.

In America we too have a word for what Israel did to prevent Hamas from playing Russian roulette with the lives of its children. We call it self-defense, as candidate Obama recognized when he stood in front of Hamas rockets in Sderot and said, "If somebody was sending rockets into my house where my two daughters sleep at night, I'm going to do everything in my power to stop that. And I would expect Israelis to do the same thing."

Alan Dershowitz
Cambridge, Massachusetts

Chapter 23
Hampshire Divests from Israel,
So Contributors Should Divest from Hampshire

On February 12, 2009 students for Justice in Palestine announced that they had persuaded Hampshire to become the first American college to divest from Israel. The story, it turns out, was a bit more complex. I immediately wrote an Op-Ed in The Jerusalem Post *and began a campaign with the following press release:*

Several months ago, a rabidly anti Israel group on the Hampshire College campus began a campaign to try to get the college to divest from six companies that they claim helped "the Israeli occupation of Palestine." Those who came up with this formulation regard all of Israel, including Tel Aviv, Haifa and Ben Gurion Airport, as "occupied Palestine." In other words, their goal is to end the existence of Israel. This divestment effort is part of an international campaign against Israel. Until now, every American university administration has categorically rejected this attempt to single out Israel in a world filled with massive human rights abusers. But Hampshire caved in to student and faculty pressure and its Board of Directors agreed to divest from these six companies along with a series of others that did not meet the standards of Hampshire College. The student group, supported by many faculty members, claimed total victory, issuing a press release that boasted that Hampshire has become the first college in the United States to divest from Israel. It urged other universities to follow its lead.

Those supporting the petition include the notorious anti-Semite Cynthia McKinney, America and Israel basher Noam Chomsky and other Israel haters. The six companies include General Electric, ITT, Motorola and other corporations that employ thousands of American workers. The divestment campaign applies to Israel and Israel alone. Hampshire will continue to deal with companies that supply Iran, Saudi Arabia, China, Cuba, North Korea, Zimbabwe, Libya, Syria, Sudan, Belarus and other brutal dictatorships around the world that routinely murder civilians, torture and imprison dissenters, deny educational opportunities to women, imprison gays and repress speech. Indeed many of those who support divestiture against Israel actively support these repressive regimes. This divestment campaign has absolutely nothing to do with human rights. It is motivated purely by hatred for the Jewish state. As *New York Times* columnist Tom Friedman put it: "Criticizing Israel is not anti-Semitic, and saying so is vital. But singling out Israel for opprobrium and international sanctions—out of proportion to any other party in the Middle East—is anti-Semitic and not saying so is dishonest."

The petition itself mentions nothing about terrorism directed against Israeli civilians, rocket attacks aimed at its kindergartens, and the unwillingness of Hamas even to recognize Israel's right to exist. It seeks to express "solidarity with Palestinian students whose access to education is severely inhibited by the Israeli occupation." It fails to add that Palestinian students have more and better access to education than Arab students in nearly every other part of the Middle East. It fails to mention that students are routinely arrested for expressing dissenting views in Iran, Saudi Arabia, Syria and other Muslim nations. It fails to mention that Israel has affirmative action programs for its Palestinian students. It fails to mention that when Israel ended the occupation of Gaza in an effort to trade land for peace, all it got in return was more than 6,000 rockets fired from Gaza at its children. It fails to present any balance concerning the Israel-Palestine conflict.

When protests over the Hampshire action began, the administration issued a statement of clarification, which did not mention Israel but claimed, obliquely, that "the decision expressly did not pertain to a political movement or single out businesses active in a specific region or country." [To read the entire statement go to: http://www. hampshire.edu/news/11271.htm]

But Hampshire President Hexter acknowledged that "it was the good work of SJP"—the virulently anti-Israel group called Student For Justice in Palestine—"that brought this issue to the attention of the committee."

They can't have it both ways. They undertook no action based on alleged violations by any country other than Israel, which allowed the anti-Israel group to claim victory, as they have been doing even after the "clarification." Virtually every media report was headlined "Hampshire First College in United States to Divest From Israel."

Before writing this article, I spoke to the President and the Chairman of the Board. They denied that this divestment action was directed against Israel. I asked them to issue a statement which made that clear: namely, "Hampshire rejected an attempt by Students for Justice in Palestine to divest from companies supporting the occupation of Palestine, and instead applied existing principles, requiring them to divest from companies which failed to meet certain standards." They refused to issue any such statement, obviously because they didn't want to alienate the anti-Israel students. Like most universities, they do want to have it both ways. They want to appear to be saying one thing to the anti-Israel students and another thing to those who would be appalled at singling out Israel for divestment. But on an issue of this kind, they simply can't have it both ways: either they rejected efforts to single out Israel for divestiture, in which case they should say so, or they accepted these efforts, and covered it up with a cosmetically-broader divestiture, which appears to be the case.

It may well be that the anti-Israel student group has hijacked the voice of the college, but if so the hijacking has not been strongly resisted. The voice of the student group has become the voice of the college because it has been clearer and less ambiguous.

My son, who went to Hampshire College, has urged me to take this action. We have supported the college through tuition payments and occasional gifts. No more! I now call on all decent people—supporters and critics of Israel alike—to make no further contributions to a school that now promotes discrimination and is complicit in evil. There must be a price paid for bigotry, and the actions of Hampshire College in singling out only Israel for divestiture is bigotry plain and simple. Silence is not an option. Inaction is not an option. Fighting back against the likes of Cynthia McKinney is mandatory for all people of good will.

The goal is not to harm the students or faculty of Hampshire College, but the petition claims that sentiment in favor of this bigoted resolution is overwhelming among students and faculty. Students and faculty too must understand that bigotry has its cost.

Hampshire College will survive its self-inflicted wound, but decency cannot survive with the kind of double standard bigotry directed only against the Jewish state.

Hampshire is a small college without much influence. But those who are conducting the national campaign see their victory at Hampshire as an opening wedge with which to get other more influential universities to follow suit by adopting similarly bigoted proposals. This is a cancer that is threatening to spread around the world, and it must be stopped where it began—at Hampshire. Until and unless the Hampshire administration clarifies its ambiguous "clarification" to make it unequivocally clear that it rejects any and all efforts to single out Israel for divestment, contributions to that otherwise fine school should be placed on hold.

In response to my Op-Ed, Hampshire's president wrote the following:

Dear Alan,

We begin by affirming our high esteem for you, both as a legal scholar and a powerful voice against anti-Semitism. We also appreciate that as a parent of a Hampshire College alumnus, you are part of a community that we hold dear. Nonetheless, we are saddened and frustrated by your recent column in the *Jerusalem Post* and elsewhere and by your many comments in the press, which present information about the actions of the Hampshire College Board of Trustees that is simply not true. Hampshire College did not divest from Israel or take the action it did because of Israel's relationship with the Palestinians or its presence on the West Bank.

At no time did the college or the board take actions or make statements motivated by anti-Semitism, bigotry and anti-Israelism. Your influence in the public sphere of ideas has the power to cause great harm to our—or, indeed, any—institution's reputation. So our frustration stems from your decision to rely not on the official statements of the board of trustees and from us as individuals, but rather from the press releases of a student group, Students for Justice in Palestine.

...

[L]et us emphasize again that this review did not include Israel, its interaction with the Palestinians, nor its presence on the West Bank as tests for the stocks in this fund. Moreover, Hampshire currently holds investments in funds that include many hundreds of companies that do business in Israel and in at least three actual Israeli companies: Amdocs, Teva Pharmaceuticals and Check Point Software.

We understand that socially responsible investing is a very powerful tool and must be used prudently. The investment committee and now the full board have recognized during this process that the college's policy on socially responsible investment, last revised in 1994, has become outdated and much too awkward to implement. We are now at work developing a new college policy on socially responsible investing, one that is up-to-date and provides clear guidance for our investment advisors.

Sadly, though, there have been students and some members of our faculty who have mischaracterized what happened here, claiming that the board did something that it did not do. None is a member of the investment committee. We have great respect for our students and encourage their endeavors—academic, social, political. We very much want our campus to be a place for learning and for healthy debate from all points of view. But we are also clear, and urge you to understand us clearly, when we say that students do not speak for the college and may not willfully misrepresent the school. It will be, and must be, the college's task to undertake any disciplinary action, according to its established rules and procedures. Discipline is an internal process that is not shared with the public.

We understand that this is an emotional issue for all involved. We simply want to state the facts plainly, separating them from the rhetoric, which, while very public, remains all too often untrue. Your good opinion matters to us; it matters, yes, because you are an influential public figure, but it matters even more because we count you as one of the Hampshire family, and hope that you will think of yourself that way, too.

And I responded:

Dear President Hexter:

I appreciate your note and your efforts to clarify the actions of Hampshire. The reality, however, is that the media and much of the world believes that Hampshire has become the first college to divest from Israel.

This perception is being used by enemies of Israel to get other universities to divest. I am deeply committed to seeing that bigoted effort fail. Neither Hampshire nor you, nor Mr. Roos has done enough to make it clear that you rejected the SJP's campaign to divest from Israel.

I can understand why you may not want to offend the majority of the student body and a significant number of faculty who support divestment from Israel, but you must do so if you do not want them to continue to be able to claim victory. So long as they can plausibly do so, there is a danger that other universities may follow suit. The proponents of the divestment must be seen by others to have lost—to have had their petition decisively rejected.

When I spoke to Mr. Roos, the chairman of the board, I predicted that the clarification would fail, even backfire. You asked for my help but rejected my advice. I would still like to work with you to resolve this zero-sum conflict. I suggest the following steps:

1. Publicly buy back the two stocks that the SJP demanded you sell that do not violate the Hampshire policy but that do business with Israel, and announce why you are buying them back.

2. Announce clearly that Hampshire rejected and will continue to reject the SJP efforts to single out Israel for divestment.

3. Announce publicly what you have said in your letter to me that those students and faculty who are claiming that Hampshire has divested from Israel are not telling the truth, are misrepresenting their authority to speak for Hampshire, and that no other school should use Hampshire's actions as a precedent for divesting from Israel.

If you take these actions it would be my honor to make a very public contribution to Hampshire to promote dialogue with regard to the Mideast.

I hope you will take seriously my efforts to work with you. If you decide to issue these statements, I would be happy to work with you on the language so as to avoid a recurrence of the failure of the prior clarification. I am confident we can resolve this if you are willing to say forthrightly in public what you have so eloquently said and written in private to me and others.

Hampshire accepted my conditions and I wrote the following:

"Hampshire has now done the right thing. It has made it unequivocally clear that it did not and will not divest from Israel. Indeed, it will continue to hold stock in companies that do business with Israel as well as with Israeli companies, so long as these companies meet the general standards that Hampshire applies to all of its holdings. As I previously wrote to President Hexter, if Hampshire did the right thing and made its position crystal clear I would urge contributors to continue to contribute to this fine school. I now do so. Indeed, I plan myself to make a contribution to Hampshire and to urge that my contribution, and perhaps others, be used to start a fund to encourage the presentation of all reasonable views regarding the Middle East to the college community. Debate about the Middle East is essential and criticism of any of the parties, when warranted, is healthy. What I condemned and continue to condemn is the singling out of Israel for divestment, unwarranted condemnation or any other sanction. I look forward to working together with Hampshire to assure that the marketplace of ideas remains open to all reasonable views on this important issue, and that students feel comfortable expressing views that may not represent the majority view on the campus."

Chapter 24
Hate Mail

In the aftermath of the Gaza conflict, my hate mail increased dramatically. I always get hate mail. I attract hate mail the way movie stars attract fan mail. For years, I have posted the "best" of my hate mail in my law school office door, so the students can get some idea of what it means to live a life of controversy.

In recent years, most of my hate mail has pertained to Israel. The mail I received during and following the war in Gaza illustrates the point I have been making about the emotional nature of the reaction to the civilians deaths induced by Hamas's tactics. Then again, virtually all the attacks on Israel are emotionally based. My friend Phyllis Chessler has noted the "almost eroticized" nature of Israel-hating.

Most of the emails are simply vile and devoid of content, such as the following:

> "What a fucking asshole you are Alan. If people treated Jews the way they treated Palestinians your screeching would be heard worldwide forever. Asshole! You stole their land and you know it dickface jew."

> Name: antijew

One particular email that I received in the aftermath of Gaza is particularly noteworthy because of the credentials of the author. Here it is in full.

> From: "Standish Lawder"
> Date: Sat, 14 Feb 2009 17:06:32 -0700
> To: <dersh@law.harvard.edu>
> Subject: From a former Harvard professor

> It was the academic year 1975-76 when I served as the Luce Professor of Film at Harvard, on leave from my position at Yale. Then I moved to the University of California at San Diego to chair the Visual Arts Dept on that campus. So clearly I am familiar with your situation within academia.

> Dear Professor, this is to say I regard you with consummate disgust. Despite your position, you are clearly scum. Why? You regard Palestinians as an inferior species. Hey, guess what? People are people. Their only sin is being born in a region of our planet that you claim to be given to Israel by God. He is not a real estate agent.

> Your life is apparently committed to the evil Israeli mission of ethnic cleansing (and yes, that's *exactly* what it is). There is no doubt that history will regard you as more evil than the Nazis.

> Please think about this (what a hopeless request!)

> In any event, I felt I had to send this message to you. What you did to Finkelstein is unconscionable. He tells the truth, and you punished him for this brave act.

> For people like me who really know (via the internet) what is really happening In the Middle East, he is a saint and you are scum.

> Once again, you disgust me. If I were ever to meet you, I would spit in your face. You are scum, consummate scum. Do I make myself clear?

> Very sincerely,

> Standish Lawder, PhD

My initial reaction was to disbelieve that so-credentialed an author could have written so crass a letter. I responded as follows:

> "An anti-Semitic nut is using your email. You should stop him. He's making you sound like David Duke."

When I determined that he really had written the email, I wrote an additional response.

> "Thank you so much for your anti-Semitic email which I will include in a book of bigoted mail I have received. Yours is particularly useful because it demonstrates that, as in Nazi Germany, credentialed academics can be as anti-Semitic as street thugs. You will be pleased that all proceeds from my book will be contributed to Israel to protect its citizens from terrorism and from bigots like you who support terrorism. Keep your bigoted emails coming. Israel can use the money.
>
> (Put this in bigot book file)

He replied with the following:

> Dear Alan,
>
> How grateful you must be for the existence of the "Anti-Semitic" label. It enables you to so easily dismiss anyone who is opposed to Israel's policy of ethnic cleansing. There is no thinking involved, no morality called into question. "You're anti-Semitic," you say and that's that. End of discussion. That a Harvard professor would use such cheap device is downright pitiful.
>
> Please try imagining your life if you could not attack with "anti-Semitic" label.
> You would be helpless without this cheap rhetorical device which prohibits further intelligent and reasoned discussion of the issue. Listen here: my children are Jewish, as is their mother. The Jews are, in many ways, wonderful people, but their insane, outrageous and unacceptable claim to be the "chosen people" is a profound insult to the other citizens of the planet. Do you not realize this? There will be no peace on this earth until Jews join the rest of the human race.
>
> But clearly I am wasting my time talking to you. I am thoroughly disgusted by your total lack of humanitarian values. You are scum. At least have the decency to include this comment in your collection of so-called "anti-Semitic" comments.

Then I replied:

> " I will certainly include your ignorant and Hitlerite comments about the Jews joining the human race as well as your pathetic defense that 'some of my best children are Jews.' You keep making my point. Write more. I can see an entire chapter devoted to your bigotry."

His next letter actually includes the defense—I'm quoting now—"and many of my best friends are Jews." Yeah, like Norman Finkelstein! Then, while denying he is an anti-Semite, he wrote as follows:

> "Our government is now in Tel Aviv. Benjamin Franklin's prophesy of 1789 is coming true: "The Jews are a danger to this land, and if they are allowed to enter, they will imperil its institutions."
>
> Most Americans don't really understand this is happening but as this truth is more and more widely realized, the groundswell of resentment will naturally be enormous. And naturally, you and your ilk will duplicitously label this totally justifiable and understandable resentment as 'anti-Semitism.' What kind of nonsense is this?"

The Franklin quote is a hoax. Among numerous historians debunking it, Franklin biographer Carl Van Doren wrote: "There is no evidence of the slightest value that Franklin ever made the alleged speech or ever said or thought anything of the kind about the Jews." The quote, however circulates on anti-Israel websites.

The Lawder letter was reminiscent of the following one I had received by an equally credentialed— and equally bigoted and ignorant—Rutgers professor in the aftermath of the Lebanon War of 2006:

> Dear Alan:
>
> You have long known been known as a rancid defender of Israeli fascism toward its Arab neighbors but this summer you wrote an article rationalizing Israeli attacks on civilians while Israel was visiting a mini-Holocaust on Lebanon. When Human Rights Watch published evidence of war crimes, you stitched together a set of lies suggesting otherwise, which lies you did not retract (of course) when they were shown to be falsehoods.
>
> Now you try to block from tenure someone who has the courage and integrity to expose your history of lies and your resemblance this summer to classic Nazi-apologists. This after earlier attempting to block publication of his work and even sliming the memory of his mother. Norman Finkelstein has integrity and intellectual quality you will never experience first-hand.
>
> Regarding your rationalization of Israeli attacks on Lebanese civilians, let me just say that if there is a repeat of Israeli butchery toward Lebanon and if you decide once again to rationalize it publicly, look forward to a visit from me. Nazis—and nazi-like apologists such as yourself-need to be confronted directly.
>
> Robert Trivers

These letters in particular have helped me to understand how so many professors and so called intellectuals could have supported and collaborated with Hitler and Stalin. Hannah Arendt was wrong when she came up with her characterization of "the banality of evil," suggesting that Nazism was built on the backs of such banal figures as Adolf Eichmann. Perhaps she did so to hide her own personal involvement with one of the least banal of all Nazis, the philosopher Martin Heidegger, with whom she had an affair. The book and film, *The Reader,* tries to make the same point. The Germans who carried out the Holocaust were illiterate women, who were more ashamed of the inability to read and write than of their murder of Jews.

The banal and bigoted mail I receive is not always written by banal street thugs—though you wouldn't know it from their threatening words. Some of the most credentialed people in the world—professors, artists, Nobel laureates—hold some of the most thoughtless, bigoted, irrational and yes, anti-Semitic views when it comes to the Jewish state. That is the sad—no evil—reality, and people of good will must understand and combat such evil regardless of its source.

Chapter 25
Defeating Freeman: A Patriotic Duty

In March 2009 Charles W. Freeman, Jr. was nominated to the important position of chairman of the National Intelligence Council. The nomination was immediately criticized by many across the political spectrum and Freeman eventually withdrew. This generated a flurry of anti-Israel criticism and attacks on the so-called Israel Lobby. I responded with the following article.

Those who successfully challenged the nomination of Charles W. Freeman, Jr. to become chairman of the National Intelligence Council should be praised for an act of high patriotism. It would have been disastrous for the United States to have, as the person responsible for overseeing "policy-neutral intelligence assessments" for the President, a zealot who is anything but policy-neutral when it comes to two of the most important areas of international conflict.

Freeman not only has extremist views regarding the Middle East and China, but he has been beholden to lobby groups that are anxious to influence intelligent assessments regarding Saudi Arabia and China. Freeman bowed out when it became clear that his highly questionable financial ties to the Saudi and China lobby would be deeply probed by inspectors general, Congressional staffers and the media. He couldn't handle the truth about his financial ties to these lobbies which do not serve the interests of the United States. The heavy thumbs of the powerful Saudi and Chinese lobbies would have subtly, and perhaps invisibly, weighed on Freeman's intelligence assessment.

Freeman is an ideologue who apparently believed that China should have been more aggressive in its crackdown on the peaceful Tiananmen Square protestors. At the same time, he has been critical of American support for Israeli efforts to stop violent terrorists from blowing up Israeli school busses and firing rockets at Israeli kindergartens. There is only one rational explanation for why a smart intelligence official would be so irrational as to express more sympathy for brutal Chinese repression of peaceful dissent than for Israeli self-defense against violent terrorism: Freeman has been bought and paid for by lobbies that he does not wish to alienate. He has a long history of playing the tunes selected for him by those who have paid him. He is an ideological zealot when it comes to the Middle East. Senator Charles Schumer correctly characterized his views as "over the top" and an "irrational hatred of Israel."

Freeman acknowledged that he is deeply and emotionally committed to a fundamental change in US policy toward Israel. That is certainly his right as a private citizen or even as an elected official. But his extremist views would not have served him, or our nation well, as the person responsible for what are supposed to be "policy-neutral intelligence assessments." An ideologue with such heavy financial baggage is simply incapable of policy-neutrality, and he should have known that.

If there was ever any doubt about his neutrality, he eliminated it by his over-the-top reaction to those who challenged his qualifications for the job based on his record. He railed against "the Israel lobby" blaming it, and it alone, for his failure to get the job. He ignored those human rights advocates who were outraged by his defense of the Chinese repression of the Tiananmen demonstrators and his unwavering support for the most repressive regime in the Middle East. He ignored environmentalists who worried that he was far too beholden to oil interests. And he ignored patriotic Americans who support U.S. policy in the Middle East because they believe it is good for America, for democracy and for the war against terrorism.

Freeman was not alone in invoking the "power" of the Israel lobby and accusing it of unpatriotic actions. He teamed up with Stephen Walt, the discredited academic who has recently made a career of blaming all of America's ills on "The Lobby." Here is how Walt gleefully put it: "For all of you out there who may have questioned whether there was a powerful 'Israel Lobby' or admitted that it existed but didn't think it had much influence...think again." Walt ignored the fact that the powerful Saudi, China and foreign oil lobbies were supporting Freeman because they believed, quite correctly, that his assessment of intelligence would be anything but neutral when it came to protecting their interests. He also ignored the fact that AIPAC—which Walt considers the puppet master of the Jewish Lobby—took no position on the Freeman nomination, and that those who opposed it included critics of Israeli policies.

So let me understand the Freeman-Walt position. When the Saudi's, the Chinese and foreign oil lobbies (with a small "l") exercise their influence, that is freedom of speech and the right to petition the government. But when the Israel Lobby (capital "L") challenges an appointment, such action is "dual loyalty," "un-American" and "unpatriotic." Their other position is that any time people of diverse backgrounds and views independently challenge a government decision that relates to the Middle East, this represents the collective action of the notorious and powerful Israel Lobby, rather than the heartfelt views of individual patriotic Americans.

Finally, they seem to believe that animosity toward Israel, without more, qualifies someone for any government of academic position, regardless of other disqualifying factors, and that anyone who challenges such an appointment—regardless of the reason—is having his strings pulled by a foreign power. This is bigotry, plain and simple.

The truth is that the Freeman appointment was bad for America, bad for peace in the Middle East, bad for human rights in China, bad for Tibet, bad for the environment, and bad for "policy-neutral intelligence." Those who challenged it performed a patriotic duty. They should be praised for helping the Obama Administration avoid a serious blunder that threatened to compromise the President's ability to act in the interest of the United States on the basis of policy-neutral intelligence. All Americans owe them a debt of gratitude.

Chapter 26
Bishop Tutu's Call For A Gaza Investigation Will Encourage More Terrorism

On March 16, 2009, a group of 16 self-described experts on "international justice and reconciliation of conflict"—including Bishop Desmond Tutu, who has characterized Israeli self-defense actions as "unchristian"—called for the establishment of "a United Nations Commission" to conduct an "independent and impartial investigation" of war crime allegations growing out of the Gaza conflict. There is of course no need to conduct any investigation of whether Hamas has committed war crimes: they readily admit—indeed they boast—that they are trying to kill as many Jewish Israeli citizens as their anti-personnel rockets are capable of killing. They also acknowledge, as a Hamas legislator did on television, that they use women and children as "human shields."

The only real target of this investigation is Israel, which, according to British military expert, Richard Kemp:

> "ha[d] very little choice other than to carry on with its military operations until it reaches the conclusion it needs which is to stop Hamas from firing rockets at its people in its territory.
>
> ...
>
> I think—I would say that from my knowledge of the IDF and from the extent to which I have been following the current operation, I don't think there has ever been a time in the history of warfare when any army has made more efforts to reduce civilian casualties and deaths of innocent people than the IDF is doing today in Gaza.
>
> ...
>
> ...Hamas, the enemy they have been fighting, has been trained extensively by Iran and by Hezbollah, to fight among the people, to use the civilian population in Gaza as a human shield.
>
> ...
>
> Hamas factor in the uses of the population as a major part of their defensive plan. So even though as I say, Israel, the IDF, has taken enormous steps...to reduce civilian casualties, it is impossible, it is impossible to stop that happening when the enemy has been using civilians as a human shield."

Only a group as skewed against Israel as this one is would regard the United Nations as capable of conducting an "independent and impartial investigation" of anything involving Israel. Such an investigation would not "help build a better peace." To the contrary, it would encourage Hamas and other terrorist groups to persist in their tactic of targeting civilians from behind human shields.

Moreover, no commission could credibly investigate what Israel *did,* unless it first set out with clarity what it believed Israel *should* have done and could have done under international law to prevent Hamas rockets from continuing to target a million Israeli civilians. A United Nations investigation of Israel—in the face of that body's absolute refusal to investigate Russia, China,

Zimbabwe, Iran and so many other countries that routinely violate human rights in an egregious manner—would constitute a major victory for the Hamas double war crime strategy. It would send a powerful message to all terrorist groups that provoking democracies into responding to attacks on its civilians will result in United Nations condemnation.

Let the international community, led by the so-called experts who signed this letter, first decide what the appropriate response is for democracies faced with attacks on its civilians by terrorists who hide behind their own civilians. Only after it is first decided, in a neutral manner, what rules of self-defense should apply to all democracies faced with terrorism by those who hide behind civilians, could an independent body then credibly apply these standards to the actions of a particular country. To conduct a witch hunt against one country, which is what any United Nations Commission would do, before articulating the neutral standards applicable to all democracies, would constitute Alice-In-Wonderland justice: Verdict first, trial to follow. That is the kind of "justice" the United Nations has typically administered when it comes to Israel.

Conclusion
Can the Whole World be Wrong About Israel?

A British university student, having observed rabid demonstrations against Israel all over the world, asked me a poignant question: Can the whole world be wrong when it condemns Israel? More recently, a prominent Spanish writer, Antonio Gala, wrote threateningly in one of Spain's leading newspapers that unless the Jewish nation curbs its "avarice," the "Jewish people will again succumb, as it has done in the past to pogroms, ghettos…, exterminations, persecutions, expulsions…. Wouldn't it do well to stop and reflect on the way the same thing always repeats itself? Or is it that the rest of the world is mistaken?"

The answer is two-fold: First, it is not the whole world that is condemning Israel, though it is most of the world. Israel's actions, in defending itself against terrorists firing rockets at its civilians, have been understood by most Americans, by many Canadians, by some Europeans and by even a few Arabs. But it is true that the vast majority of people around the world engage in knee-jerk condemnation of Israel whenever it engages in self-defense—and even when it does nothing but exist. To the extent that most of the world engages in such automatic demonization of the Jewish state, the answer to the student's question is clear: Yes, when it comes to Israel, the world can be—and often is—wrong. Completely wrong. Immorally wrong. Sometimes anti-Semitically wrong.

This should come as no surprise to anyone familiar with Jewish history: for more than 1,000 years, the whole world—at least the whole Christian world—believed that Jews ritually murdered Christian children to get their blood for use in the making of Passover matza. Now, much of the Arab and Muslim world believe the blood libel. But regardless of how widespread these anti-Semitic views may be, they are simply as wrong, as the widespread view, through most of human history, that the sun revolves around the earth or that the universe is 6,000 years old.

So is the view that Israel was at fault in the actions it took in Gaza after years of allowing Hamas rockets to play Russian roulette with the lives of its children. Right and wrong—whether factual or moral—are not determined by public opinion polls. In 2003, a European Commission survey found that 59% of Europeans regarded Israel as the greatest threat to world peace, ahead of rogue states like Iran and North Korea.[15] And a study conducted by the Anti-Defamation League in late 2008 and early 2009 revealed that 31% of Europeans blamed Jews for the global financial and economic crisis.[16] These poll results tell us more about Europe than about Israel, or Jews.

The pervasive ignorance among many European and American students regarding basic facts—for example, who started the 1948 and 1967 wars? What were the Palestinians offered by the Clinton-Barak proposals of 2000–2001? When did the rocket attacks against Israeli civilians begin?—is staggering.

Some have been indoctrinated by radical professors such as Harvard Law School's Duncan Kennedy, who, despite his lack of expertise on the Middle East or in international law, teaches a course called "Israel/Palestine Legal Issues." Kennedy recently wrote an Op-Ed in the *Harvard Crimson* telling students that a "consensus of 'informed observers'" believed Israel was to blame for the Gaza conflict.[17] Few students are prepared to stand up to professors, though in this case third-year law student Joel Pollak penned a cogent response, pointing out that Kennedy's article was "filled with errors few undergraduates would make," and adding: "Undergraduates may err, but it takes a tenured professor to distort reality that badly."[18]

There is much willful blindness regarding the facts and figures of the Gaza War. During the war, Hamas put out false information and exaggerated figures that were immediately accepted by much of the media and many human rights groups. Evidence of such distortion was, according to a report in the *Jerusalem Post:*

> provided by Col. Moshe Levi, the head of the IDF's Gaza Coordination and Liaison Administration (CLA), which compiled the IDF figures.
>
> As an example of such distortion, he cited the incident near a UN school in Jabalya on January 6, in which initial Palestinian reports falsely claimed IDF shells had hit the school and killed 40 or more people, many of them civilians.
>
> In fact, he said, 12 Palestinians were killed in the incident—nine Hamas operatives and three noncombatants. Furthermore, as had since been acknowledged by the UN, the IDF was returning fire after coming under attack, and its shells did not hit the school compound.
>
> > "From the beginning, Hamas claimed that 42 people were killed, but we could see from our surveillance that only a few stretchers were brought in to evacuate people," said Levi, adding that the CLA contacted the PA Health Ministry and asked for the names of the dead. "We were told that Hamas was hiding the number of dead."
>
> As a consequence of the false information, he added, the IDF was considering setting up a "response team" for future conflicts whose job would be to collect information, analyze it and issue reports as rapidly as possible that refuted Hamas fabrications.

The IDF has now also identified 580 combatants who were killed in the fighting and estimates that two-thirds of the 320 bodies yet to be identified were those of "terror operatives." Many others, who were classified as non-combatants, were human shields such as wives and children of Nizar Rayyan, a Hamas military commander who refused to allow his family to leave his home even after he was warned by Israel that it would be bombed.[19]

Ignorance is the father and mother of bigotry. It is also its child. Because emotion based on prejudice rather than reason based on information often drives the reaction to Israel, many anti-Israel agitators deliberately dumb it down, substituting slogans for facts, chanting for thinking and bigotry for fairness. Remarkably, much of this occurs on university campuses, orchestrated by hard-left professors who see their mission as propagandizing for the most radical elements of the Palestinian movement, rather than as teaching critical thinking or conveying unbiased information.

Many of these rabidly anti-Israel polemicists are Jewish—at least on their parent's side. Some are Israelis—or Israeli expatriates living in Europe or America. They use their Jewish heritage or Israeli citizenship as phony credibility chips. In effect, they offer an opposite, but equally irrational, version of the argument ad hominem: "Consider our arguments not on their merits or demerits, but on the basis of who is offering them." Or put more bluntly: "We are Jews—or Israelis. If even we demonize Israel, it must indeed be demonic." As Norman Finkelstein, who has characterized the Jewish nation as satanic, recently told the *Tehran Times:* "I think Israel ... is becoming an insane state. And we have to be honest about that... It is a lunatic state."[20]

Constructive criticism of Israel and its policies is healthy. It is ongoing in Israel and among its supporters throughout the world. Demonizing the Jewish state or subjecting its actions to a double standard is wrong and must be answered in the marketplace of ideas. That is why I wrote and published the material in this short book. I will continue to fight against those who would destroy Israel—by rockets, suicide bombs, nuclear weapons, falsehoods, bigotry, divestments, boycotts or any other means—as long as I have the strength to do so.

[15] European Commission, "Iraq and Peace in the World," Flash Eurobarometer survey, Nov. 2003, < http://europa.eu.int/comm/public_opinion/flash/fl151_iraq_full_report.pdf>.

[16] Anti-Defamation League, "ADL Survey in Seven European Countries Finds Anti-Semitic Attitudes Steady; 31 Percent Blame Jews for Financial Crisis," Press Release, Feb. 10, 2009, < http://www.adl.org/PresRele/ASInt_13/5465_13.htm>.

[17] Duncan Kennedy, "A Context For Gaza," Harvard Crimson, Feb. 2, 2009, <http://www.thecrimson.com/article.aspx?ref=526273>.

[18] Joel Pollak, "Tenured But Wrong," Harvard Crimson, Feb. 4, 2009, <http://www.thecrimson.com/article.aspx?ref=526318>.

[19] Yaakov Katz, ibid.

[20] Norman Finkelstein, quoted in Selcuk Guitasli, "Israel is committing a holocaust in Gaza: Norman Finkelstein," Tehran Times, Feb. 19, 2009, <http://tehrantimes.com/index_View.asp?code=189330>.